CELESTIAL FREQUENCIES
ORACLE CARDS AND HEALING ACTIVATORS

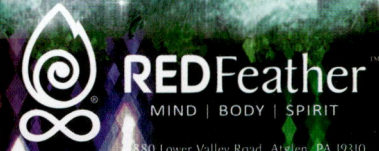

Other REDFeather Titles by the Author:
Magical Dimensions Oracle Cards and Activators, ISBN 978-0-7643-5345-1

Other REDFeather Titles on Related Subjects:
Sacred Geometry Healing Cards, Phoenix Gateway's Emily Kisvarda, ISBN 978-0-7643-5710-7

Shamanic Healing Oracle Cards, Michelle A. Motuzas, ISBN 978-0-7643-5036-8

Copyright © 2022 by Susan Goldwag (Lightstar)

Library of Congress Control Number: 2021948668

All rights reserved. No part of this work may be reproduced or used in any form or by any means—graphic, electronic, or mechanical, including photocopying or information storage and retrieval systems—without written permission from the publisher.

The scanning, uploading, and distribution of this book or any part thereof via the Internet or any other means without the permission of the publisher is illegal and punishable by law. Please purchase only authorized editions and do not participate in or encourage the electronic piracy of copyrighted materials.

"Red Feather Mind Body Spirit" logo is a trademark of Schiffer Publishing, Ltd.
"Red Feather Mind Body Spirit Feather" logo is a registered trademark of Schiffer Publishing, Ltd.

Type set in Lightfoot/Mulan/Chaparral Pro

ISBN: 978-0-7643-6372-6
Printed in China

Published by REDFeather Mind, Body, Spirit
An imprint of Schiffer Publishing, Ltd.
4880 Lower Valley Road
Atglen, PA 19310
Phone: (610) 593-1777; Fax: (610) 593-2002
Email: Info@redfeathermbs.com
Web: www.redfeathermbs.com

For our complete selection of fine books on this and related subjects, please visit our website at www.redfeathermbs.com. You may also write for a free catalog.

REDFeather Mind Body Spirit's titles are available at special discounts for bulk purchases for sales promotions or premiums. Special editions, including personalized covers, corporate imprints, and excerpts, can be created in large quantities for special needs. For more information, contact the publisher.

We are always looking for people to write books on new and related subjects. If you have an idea for a book, please contact us at proposals@schifferbooks.com.

The intent of the author is only to offer information of a general nature to help you in your spiritual endeavors. In the event you use the information in this book for yourself, which is your constitutional right, the author and publisher assume no responsibility for your actions.

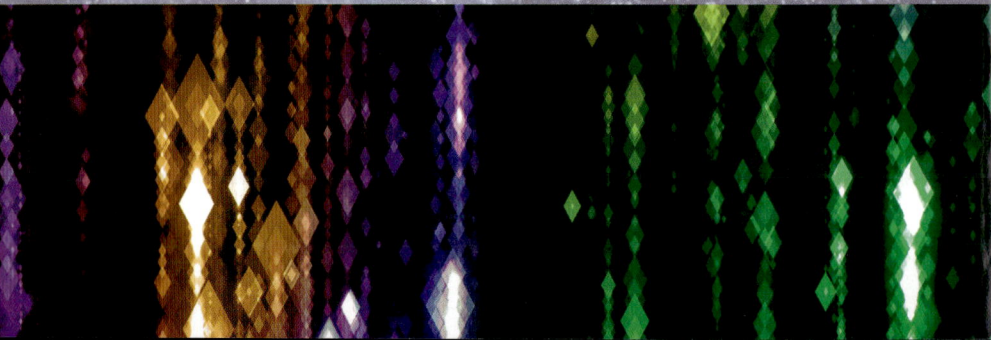

"Wow! I absolutely love this beautiful oracle activator deck; the art is amazing. The vibrational frequency levels encompassed within the cards opens multidimensional communication and healing on a deep soul level. There is a depth of wisdom within the presence of Celestial Frequencies. I feel alchemical healing and visual activation in action while working with the inspirational Galactic and Celestial Beings, Healing Shields, and Healing Codes through the Healing Activator Grids, as suggested in the guidebook. I feel as though I am traveling the landscapes of the universe on such a deep soul level as I focus on receiving clarity! I love the way you can incorporate using both decks together . . . truly food for the soul. . . . Magical Dimensions meets Celestial Frequencies for inspiration, health and well-being."

—Donna Lee

"Lightstar, I love, love, love this deck! Much like a photo from the highest peaks of Sedona can't possibly capture the true beauty, wonder, and essence your eye beholds, I cannot begin to convey in words the unlimited potential of what you managed to bring forth and package for us in a small box. Lightstar, you are a treasure and you have created a priceless gem for all inspired to pick up your deck. I am just mind blown!!! The Celestial Frequencies and Oracle Activation by Lightstar soars right past "NEXT LEVEL" and launches you onward as far as you are ready and willing to go . . . UNLIMITED POTENTIAL! I am so enthralled with the Pyramid Builder Spread, which I utilized for insight on several Passion Projects of mine. The energies, insights, and wisdom that came through so resonate, validate, and inspire me to laser-focus my intent where it truly supports and fuels the collective mission of all I aspire to bring forth. It basically wrote my mission statement for each project. Thank you, Lightstar, for being an angelic conduit. The beauty and energy of the artwork alone is priceless. I have never seen another deck incorporate art, colors, sound frequencies, healing codes, and so much more within them. You can't help but elevate your consciousness every time you open the box. Thank you! Thank you! Thank you!"

—Shelley Evans, founder, Ultimate Light Mission

"I am so grateful to have the opportunity to have this magnificent Celestial Frequencies oracle deck. The cards are absolutely beautiful, and I resonate with them on such a deep soul level. They contain so much information, and as I handle them I can feel the connection to the Light Beings almost instantly. I have done several of the oracle spreads and have received clear and accurate messages from all of them. Having worked in the past with Lightstar's beautiful Activation Codes, I love that so many of these cards are also Activators, and I plan to purchase a second deck to set up the Activation Healing Grids. I have been using the Magical Dimensions oracle deck for some time and am now using the two decks together. They work beautifully as one to access energy and messages from all of the dimensions.
Thank you Lightstar for creating these wonderful, magical, healing Oracle Cards and Healing Activators. In Love and Light!"

—Cherry Hicks

"As a professional in the transformation industry, I hold the highest regard for Lightstar's artistic creations. My Starseed clients and I love, Love, LOVE her Celestial Frequencies Oracle Cards and Healing Activators deck. The level of guidance, clarity, activation, and clearing is sublime. The new spreads are fun and interactive with all-new Celestial and Galactic beings to overfill your joy cup! One client in wide-eyed amazement offered, 'Oh my God, it's like this deck was made JUST for me!' Another jubilantly exclaimed, 'It's like having my Galactic Council RIGHT HERE with me; I'm so grateful—it's Brilliant!' I couldn't agree more. Lightstar has created a simple and fun-to-use deck that places the power of a professional reading, filled with insights, clarity, clearing (healing), activators and upgrades, greater awareness, guidance (and way more!), in your own hands. It's serious light tech made for the New Earth and all who desire to expand their consciousness and explore, to discover their inner being. What more could you want in a deck? Lightstar has raised the bar for all Oracle decks."

—Tina Campbell, owner, Divine Source Light Code

ABOUT LIGHTSTAR

Creator, Author, and Artist of the *Celestial Frequencies and Magical Dimensions* Oracle Decks

Lightstar is an internationally acclaimed, pioneering high-frequency attunement artist and celestial channel. Her enchanting and cosmic artwork is infused with sacred color rays and light codes that transmit pure Divine inspiration. Lightstar's captivating artwork has been publicized worldwide, and she has been a featured artist at galleries and venues nationwide. She serves as a spiritual catalyst for individuals to discover their gifts and realign to their natural state. Lightstar's unique Light Language Music Activation includes *special encoded healing frequencies*, designed to cleanse, shift, inspire, calm, energize, transform, and upgrade consciousness to a higher vibration! Her groundbreaking healing tools assist those who are feeling disconnected from their higher guidance, to realign with their soul, be inspired, and recall their destiny path. Lightstar also speaks a multitude of Universal Light Languages, which transmit and activate soul memories and healing codes. *Visit her website at lightstarcreations.com*

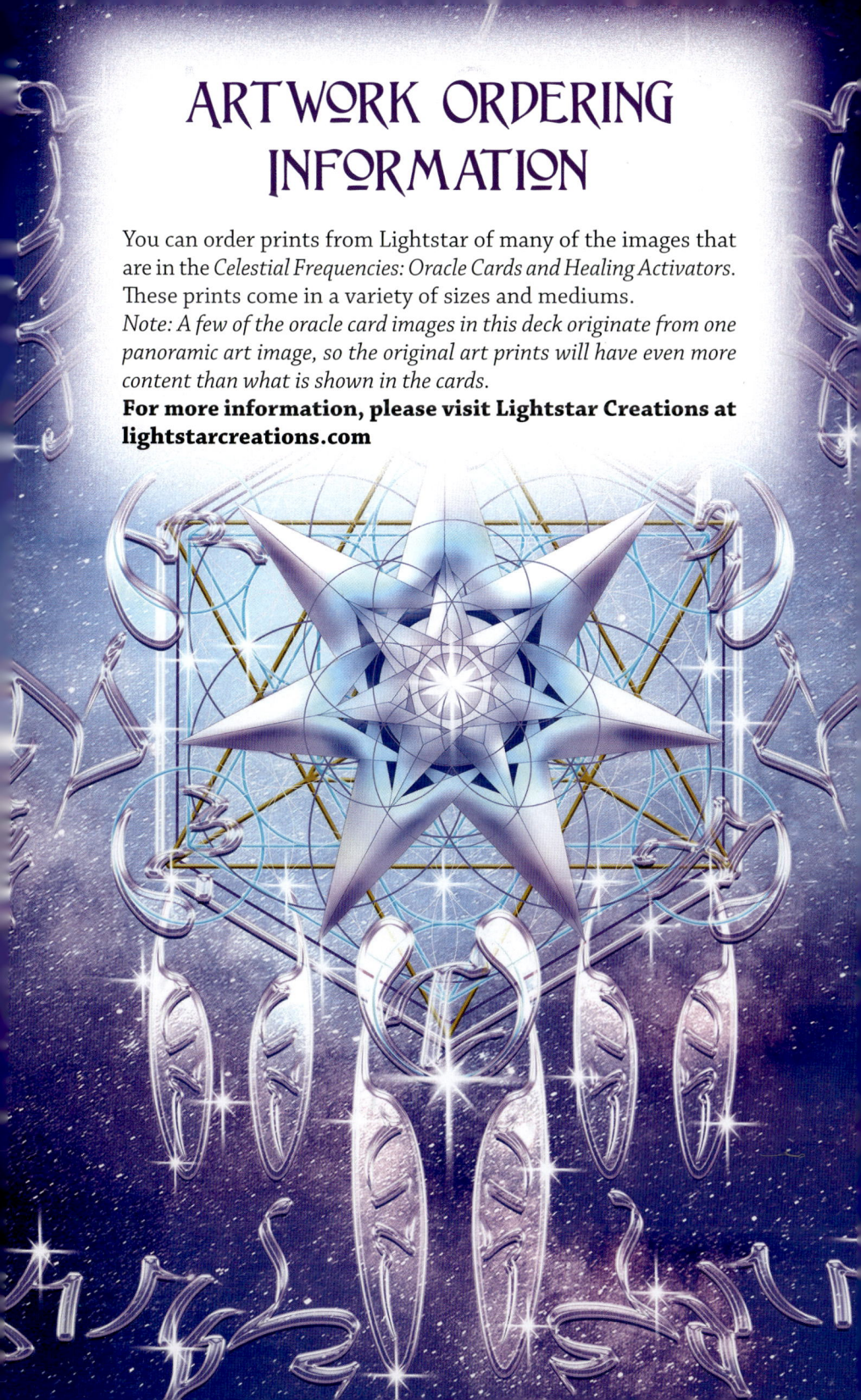

ARTWORK ORDERING INFORMATION

You can order prints from Lightstar of many of the images that are in the *Celestial Frequencies: Oracle Cards and Healing Activators*. These prints come in a variety of sizes and mediums.

Note: A few of the oracle card images in this deck originate from one panoramic art image, so the original art prints will have even more content than what is shown in the cards.

For more information, please visit Lightstar Creations at lightstarcreations.com

Celestial Frequencies Oracle Cards and Healing Activators Guidebook

lightstarcreations.com

May you be energized and activated with beautiful cosmic connections and healing frequencies to accelerate your spiritual progression, raise your frequency, and infuse your consciousness with insight, clarity, and brilliance.

~ Lightstar

Gratitude for This Project

A very special thank-you to The Creator and all the Galactic Families, Angels, Ascended Masters, Elementals, and Fairies that have brought their healing energies in cocreation of this precious oracle deck. You are my inspiration, and I am eternally grateful to share this gift with the world.

I wish to thank my beloved Standswithbear for being my muse while creating this project. I am eternally grateful for your loving heart, your encouragement, and your endless support of my artwork. It means the world to me! Thank you for your generous, brilliant, inspirational, and loving soul!

A special thank you to Ryk Hall (aka BlueStar), and Douglas Lerner, for being the inspiration for my creation of the activating Guardian Sacred Builder, and Cellular Intelligence.

And thank you to all of my amazing fans and supporters of my work and art. You inspire me in all ways.

~ *Lightstar*

Contents

Foreword and Introduction 10
Overview of the Main Card Categories 14
Cleansing and Care of Your New Deck 24
Obtaining Guidance from Your Deck 28
Unique Oracle Card Spreads 30
Healing Activator Grids 42

Oracle Card Interpretations

1 ◆ Reconnection, *Universal Healing Shield* 56
2 ◆ Innocence, *Unicorn Love* 58
3 ◆ Inspiration, *Cassiopeia Inspiration* 60
4 ◆ Acceleration, *417 Hz Cleansing Healing Code* 62
5 ◆ Transitions, *Karmic Timeweaver* 64
6 ◆ Boundaries, *Empath Healing Shield* 66
7 ◆ Perceptivity, *Psychic Healing Shield* 68
8 ◆ Sovereignty, *Orion Magical Creation* 70
9 ◆ Consciousness, *Ascension Healing Shield* 72
10 ◆ Decisiveness, *Sirius Solar Empowerment* 74
11 ◆ Love, *Pleiades Star Angel* 76
12 ◆ Expansion, *741 Hz Enlighten Healing Code* 78
13 ◆ Discernment, *Vega Fearless Journey* 80
14 ◆ Disclosure, *The Atlantean Libraries* 82
15 ◆ Compassion, *639 Hz Love Healing Code* 84

16 ◆ Wonderment, *Orb Healing* 86
17 ◆ Rejuvenation, *Purification Healing Shield* 88
18 ◆ Initiation, *Valion The Wisdom Keeper* 90
19 ◆ Solutions, *Galactic Dreamstar* 92
20 ◆ Resilience, *Lyra Genesis Activation* 94
21 ◆ Nourishment, *Gift of The Merpeople* 96
22 ◆ Focused, *Guardian Sacred Builder* 98
23 ◆ Confidence, *The Atlantean Libraries* 100
24 ◆ Magnetism, *Telos Crystal Avatar* 102
25 ◆ Innovative, *Andromeda Healing Matrix* 104
26 ◆ Participation, *Elven Alchemy* 106
27 ◆ Curiosity, *Zeta Spiritual Expansion* 108
28 ◆ Playful, *Magical Faerie Pools* 110
29 ◆ Rebalance, *Astral Healing Shield* 112
30 ◆ Success, *396 Hz Freedom Healing Code* 114
31 ◆ Upgrades, *Lightbody Spectra* 116
32 ◆ Recalibration, *Guardian Healing Shield* 118
33 ◆ Enlightenment, *Enlightened Mastery* 120
34 ◆ Courageous, *Transcending Fear* 122
35 ◆ Repair, *528 Hz Miracles Healing Code* 124
36 ◆ Infinite, *Arcturus InfinityMind* 126
37 ◆ Metamorphosis, *852 Hz Clarity Healing Code* 128
38 ◆ Integration, *Higher Self Integration* 130
39 ◆ Transmutation, *Cellular Intelligence* 132
40 ◆ Reflectivity, *The Atlantean Libraries* 134
41 ◆ Unification, *963 Hz Oneness Healing Code* 136
42 ◆ Collaboration, *The Alliance* 138
43 ◆ Enhancement, *The Etheric Med Team* 140
44 ◆ Receptivity, *Angelic Diamond Light* 142

FOREWORD AND INTRODUCTION
ENTER INTO THE CELESTIAL FREQUENCIES

Since the creation of my first oracle deck, the *Magical Dimensions Oracle Cards and Activators*, I have embarked upon a most magnificent journey further into the multidimensional dimensions and have been initiated with increased light codes. It is with great honor I present to the world this brilliant new addition, the *Celestial Frequencies: Oracle Cards and Healing Activators*. In this very special oracle deck, you will experience Divine Light Code activation and guidance from the realms of the advanced Galactic Alliances, Angels, Elementals, and Ascended Healing Masters. They will be assisting you on your spiritual path, helping you traverse beyond the density of our Earth, and into a more enlightened state of being.

I have observed that, although my name is shown on the cover of the box and guidebook of the *Magical Dimensions Oracle Cards and Activators*, many people still do not realize that I am indeed the sole artist and creator of all the images. So, yes, I am the original artist and creator of both oracle decks. Although, having said that, I do give most of the credit to The Creator, working through my human vessel to create these powerful images.

ARE THEY ORACLE OR HEALING ACTIVATORS?

If you are the proud owner of my *Magical Dimensions Oracle Cards and Activators*, then you'll already be familiar with the different types of readings, layouts, and spreads you can do. The same holds true for the *Celestial Frequencies* oracle deck as well. For those who are experiencing this deck for the first time, you will be able to use this deck as oracle cards for card readings, and you will also be able to additionally use them as what I call "Healing Activator Grids." I will explain how you can utilize this deck in a variety of layouts and spreads that will be helpful in providing insights and healing for a wide range of life circumstances.

HIGHLIGHTS OF THE DECK

It will be helpful to think of my *Celestial Frequencies* oracle deck as an intermediate intuitive tool, whereas my *Magical Dimensions Oracle Cards and Activators* is more of the starter oracle deck. There are different themes in *Celestial Frequencies*, which includes a variety of symbols, light language, and divine codes meant to stretch you beyond your psychic comfort zone. Think rubber band! However, if you already have my *Magical Dimensions Oracle Cards and Activators*, and you would like to expand upon that deck . . . the **Celestial Frequencies oracle can also be integrated and blended with that deck.** This will provide a much more enhanced and expanded oracle reading for yourself or your clients and will also enrich your experience with the Healing Activator Grids as well.

The oracle cards in this deck are categorized into several main frequency types: **Galactic and Celestial Energies, Ascended Masters and Integrative Healers, Healing Shields, Healing Codes, and other energetic cards sprinkled with Angelic and Elemental frequencies.** The Healing Shields and Healing Codes will be discussed more in depth in the following segments, since they carry enhanced frequencies and some of them will relate to the chakra / portal energy systems. These cards are all profoundly effective at providing activation, awakening, and healing.

THE KEY ENERGIES AND ORACLE INTERPRETATIONS

This guidebook contains 44 numbered card images with one main card title and one subtitle to assist with your interpretations of the cards. In my *Magical Dimensions Oracle Cards and Activators*, I included extra guidance by providing descriptive subtitles on the cards. But, with the *Celestial Frequencies: Oracle Cards and Healing Activators*, you now have ample leeway to explore even further and extract your own interpretations more freely.

Having said this, you'll not be left hanging if you need more assistance with interpretations of the cards. I do include further descriptions on each card interpretation page that are split into two sections that will list "The Key Energies" and "The Oracle Interpretation," so that way you can understand the card's meaning from both perspectives.

Additionally, I include the original artwork title of each image, which is listed on the cards, as well as the interpretation pages in this guidebook. These subtitles amplify the frequencies of the cards by containing the original art template encodements and will also assist with your card readings and Healing Activator Grids by aligning with those originally intended codes. If you find yourself particularly gravitating toward certain cards and would like to purchase a print of that particular image, you'll be able to locate the original art title that is shown on each individual card, as well as the associated description page, so you can more easily locate them on my website. If you find one or more of the card images "calling" to you repeatedly, it usually means that it will be beneficial to obtain those images and place them in your environment (as an art print) or meditate with them, so you can integrate the frequencies of that image more frequently and directly. Check my website for the options about obtaining art prints.

All of the card interpretations and resources are provided for your convenience and assistance, but please do not let this limit you in extrapolating your own meanings for the cards. **This deck is intended to strengthen your intuition, so if you receive a psychic impression that differs from the card meaning that is written . . . by all means . . . trust your intuition on this.** I am sharing the translations that were transmitted via my Celestial sources and my own psychic impressions for these cards. However, my goal is to empower you so you can recognize your own mastery, so I encourage you to explore this deck as a journey of self-discovery. Feel free to interpret the cards with what resonates best with you.

HELPFUL REALIGNMENT RESOURCES

At the end of each card description page in this guidebook, you will find a third section that provides resources as helpful realignments regarding the specific card energies. This is an expansion of what I had included in the *Magical Dimensions Oracle* (which has suggested companion crystals and an associated essential oil). Now, in the *Celestial Frequencies* oracle deck, you have an even-greater and more extensive list of helpful realigning energies. Not only do these suggestions include crystals and even more essential oils, but you'll also find realignment suggestions linked with specific types of body, mind, and spirit therapies; incense for smudging; specific flower essences; and color infusions. All of these resources are frequency specific to each card, relating to a variety of healing tools, systems, and ways to rebalance and enhance your spiritual, mental, physical, and emotional energies.

When you choose a particular card, hold it in your hand, and you can combine the associated crystal, essential oil, flower essence, therapy, or any of the suggestions listed that are most suited to match, and it will assist you with increasing the frequency of that associated card. Hold the card and diffuse or inhale the essential oils, smudge with the recommended aromatic, or merely place the card in the midst of your chosen alignment therapy. The card frequencies will then be enhanced by those particular realignments. In some cases, you may experience a healing or release when combining these in unison with one another. The combinations will help you connect more clearly with the associated subject matter of the card itself. These special enhancements help strengthen your connections with your Higher Self, the Galactics, Celestial Beings, Elementals, Angelic Realms, Ascended Masters, and Spiritual Guides.

Remember that what you focus on ultimately manifests in your reality, so you can also utilize the realignment assistance in concert with the cards to clarify and affirm what you would like to magnetize in your life. Feel free to experiment with other realignments or alternative therapies that you feel are appropriate for working with the cards themselves. There are many other types of energy frequencies that can enhance the quality of your experiences. Use your intuition to provide you with other solutions that can help you gain further insights into your own situations, or for client readings. Most of all, have lots of fun with this!

OVERVIEW OF THE MAIN CARD CATEGORIES
THE OVERVIEW

I wish to provide you with an overview of the main frequencies of the cards, so you can learn the basis of their origins, and the dimensions in which the energetic vibrations emanate from.

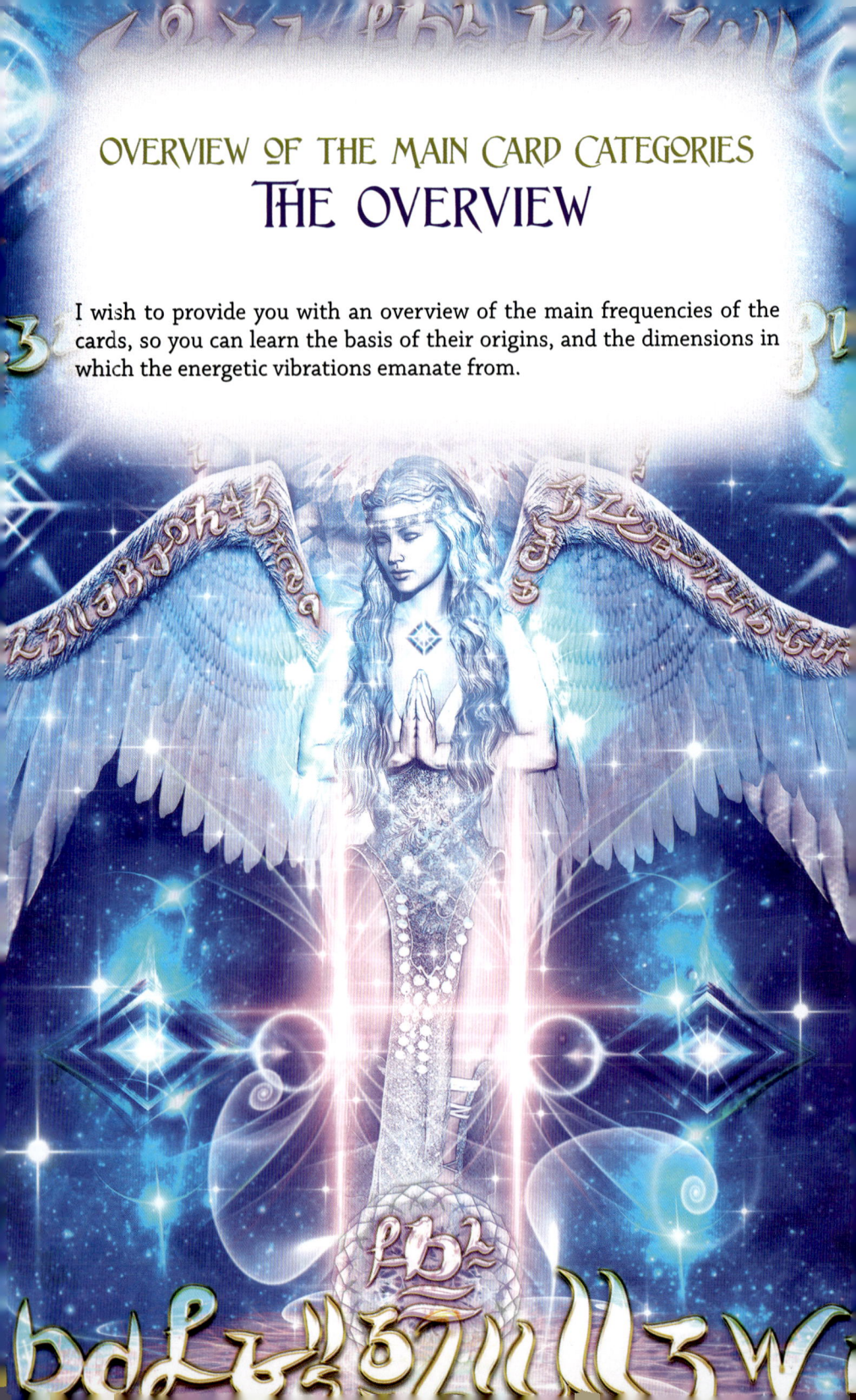

CARD DESIGNATOR ICONS

In the bottom right-hand corner of each oracle card, you'll notice different icons. There are four icons that reference the specific designation of each card in association to the four main categories of this deck. This makes it easy to separate them out of the deck when you wish to work with specific energies, or when running Healing Activator Grids or specific spreads.

Here is a guide to these four specific icons:

There are 12 cards that are associated with the Master Galactics. The seven-pointed star icon designates that these cards are linked with the Master Galactic Energies.

There are seven cards that are associated with the Healing Shields. The shield icon designates that these cards are linked with the specific Healing Shields of the deck.

There are seven cards that are associated with the Healing Codes. The code icon designates that these cards are linked with the specific Healing Codes of the deck.

The remaining 18 cards are associated with mystical influences from various beings in other dimensions and realms. The Metatron's Cube icon designates that these cards are linked with other inspirational beings, which could be either Ascended Masters, Angelics, Elementals, Fae, Cosmic, Healers, or other energies that are present in the deck.

GALACTIC AND CELESTIAL BEINGS

Although there are a variety of realms that are depicted in this deck, you'll notice that the *Celestial Frequencies* oracle deck does seem to have two main foci: the galactic realms and healing. Yes, extraterrestrials do exist. You may even be among them, oh brilliant starseed. But that's for another book, or a private session. LOL! This oracle deck's content does lean toward those who are interested in the galactic/cosmic realms, and for those who identify with being starseed or starborn. However, that is not to exclude those who may consider themselves more as a Lightworker, Lightwarrior, Earth Keeper, Shaman, Priestess, Healer, Ascension Guide, or anything else you may identify with along those lines. This deck is for anyone who feels a gravitational pull toward the deck or is guided to work with these energies. For those not as familiar with starseed material, you will be introduced to a variety of cosmic beings through this deck, and you just might find them becoming some of your best friends. You might even discover that you are indeed starborn just by awakening to the energies of this oracle deck. Wink, wink!

You will notice that 12 cards in this deck are very specifically depicting galactic races, and it is important to note that the emphasis should be placed on the energies that emanate from the image content, so try not to get locked into the belief system that ALL races from one particular star constellation appear to look the same physically. For example, not all of the extraterrestrials from Lyra look to be in the manner that I have depicted in the card artwork. There are definitely going to be variations in the cosmic realms. However, what IS important is for you to attune more fully with the vibrations and frequencies of the card itself, and to use your intuition to gain further insights into the questions you are postulating with your inquiries and activation layouts.

Since this is not a Tarot deck, I would not refer to these 12 cards as "Major Arcana." However, I would view them more as "Master Galactic Energies" that have a great impact on the other cards in the deck. They work in unison with the other cards in the deck, not in domination of them. So, for example, if you pull two cards from the deck and you picked card #11 and card #33, this does not mean that just because you have chosen card #11, with Master Galactic Energies of the Pleiades, and the other card, #33, is a depiction of the Ascended Master Realms, that card #11 trumps #33, or vice versa. There is no domination over the other. The perspectives and insights of the Master Galactic Energies fuse with the other cards, so your intuitive interpretation can be more expanded and complete.

As for the other main focus of this deck, healing, there are a variety of ways that you can gain the most out of this special oracle deck. The deck includes infused energies that are very healing in nature. In order to extract these healing vibrations, you can place your focus on whatever card(s) you are gravitating toward, and just receive the healing frequencies from them. The healing properties emanate from all the cards; however, there are a few special types of cards called "Healing Shields" and "Healing Codes" that are very special, and I'd like to explain further about these special frequencies.

THE HEALING SHIELDS

There are seven cards in this deck that I call "Healing Shields." These beautiful and potent infused shields are super powerful and packed with activation! Each one of the images is attuned to a specific realm: *Cosmic, Physical, Mental, Emotional, Dimensional, Galactic, or Spiritual*. Specific frequency codes are embedded and **INcoded** within the Healing Shields, so they are very activating and will assist you with up-leveling and upgrading your energy frequencies to a higher octave! When your oracle reading unveils one or more of the Healing Shields, you'll know that you are working with high frequencies that will help *empower or re-empower* the situation you are inquiring about. Notice that in the list below, all the descriptions begin with "re," such as "reignite, rejuvenate," etc. This is because the Healing Shields are asking you to carefully review areas in your life where some level of rebalancing is needed in order to return to a state of homeostasis. Healing Shields can surface for any one of your inquiries: health concerns, relationships, career-based issues, geographical moves; whatever the case may be. When you get these cards in your readings, it will usually prompt some type of action on your (or your client's) part, to rebalance the situation. You can also use any of these cards as Healing Activators as well. I have also included some wonderful Activator Grids in this guidebook to work with the energies of the Healing Shields even further.

Here is a quick, at-a-glance list of the energies and extra guidance for interpreting and working with the Healing Shields:

HEALING SHIELDS:
1. *Reconnection*, UNIVERSAL HEALING SHIELD
To assist with **reconnection** and alignment with your Higher Self and directly to Creator Source
Associated with the COSMIC REALMS

17. Rejuvenation, PURIFICATION HEALING SHIELD
To help with **rebalancing** the third dimension, clearing toxins, cellular nourishment, and reclaiming abundance and prosperity codes
Linked to the PHYSICAL REALMS

7. Perceptivity, PSYCHIC HEALING SHIELD
To initiate and **reignite** intuitive abilities, heighten extra sensory perception, and shield from psychic attack
Linked to the MENTAL REALMS

6. Boundaries, EMPATH HEALING SHIELD
To support and **reestablish** healthy emotional boundaries, strengthen the bioenergetic field, and dissolve emotional toxicity
Linked to the EMOTIONAL REALMS

29. Rebalance, ASTRAL HEALING SHIELD
To **reorganize** and harmonize scattered or fragmented energies in the astral, auric, and etheric realms
Linked to the DIMENSIONAL REALMS

32. Recalibration, GUARDIAN HEALING SHIELD
To **reignite** and activate multidimensional communication with galactic family, starseed alliances, and celestial purpose
Linked to the GALACTIC REALMS

9. Consciousness, ASCENSION HEALING SHIELD
To **restore** and deepen spiritual connections with the angelic realms, spiritual guides, and ascended masters
Linked to the SPIRITUAL REALMS

A Note about Reversals for Healing Shields

I typically do not include an abundance of shadow-based cards in my decks, but for those of you who like to dive into the areas of shadow work, having some reversals can be very helpful and can provide more flexibility for you in your readings. Although I do not provide specific guidance or interpretations for reversal or challenge cards, if your card pick displays one or more of the Healing Shield cards upside down, you could view that particular Healing Shield with a reverse meaning. This is not mandatory, of course, but you have the option for this if it helps clarify your reading. So, feel free to utilize the Healing Shields in this capacity as you wish. The upright positions of the Healing Shield cards already indicate that something needs to be rebalanced. However, if you get a reversal and want to read it more as a reversal or challenge, go deeper into what the shadow side is uncovering about your initial inquiry. Use your intuition to help you go into further clarification on what that particular Shield(s) properties are, and what might be required in order to bring oneself or the situation back into balance.

The Healing Codes

There are also seven cards in this deck that I call "Healing Codes." The Healing Codes resonate to specific Solfeggio tones and contain visual-activation properties. Solfeggio frequencies make up the ancient six-tone scale thought to have been used in sacred music, including the beautiful and well-known Gregorian chants. The chants and their special tones were believed to impart spiritual blessings when sung in harmony. Each Solfeggio tone is composed of a frequency required to balance your energy and keep your body, mind, and spirit in perfect unison. Experiencing the vibration of these frequencies in the form of visual art enhances these tones and can create an alchemical healing activation for the soul. You can view these Healing Codes as pure tones of insight. They represent the positive abilities within all of us to rise to the highest vision of ourselves.

Resonance with Chakras

These Healing Codes also coincide with our seven main chakra systems. There are indeed many more chakras than just seven, but for the purpose of this deck I connect them with the seven main chakras we are most aware of on the planet at this time: *Root, Sacral, Solar, Heart, Throat, Third Eye, and Crown*. One thing to note is that as many of you will know, in my *Magical Dimensions Oracle*, I utilized the word "portal" in place of the word "chakra" for the seven chakra cards in that deck. These terms are synonymous with one another; however, I still prefer the term "portal" to the latter, since I feel it is a clearer representation of what our chakra systems really are. But again, that content might be for another book entirely!

Healing Codes vs. Portals

One distinction that I would like to make is in regard to the differences between these Healing Codes and the seven portals / chakra cards in the *Magical Dimensions* oracle deck. Since I have created this *Celestial Frequencies* oracle deck to be either a stand-alone *or* an extension and upgrade to the *Magical Dimensions* oracle, then you can also view the Healing Codes as upgrades to the portal cards in the *Magical Dimensions* oracle. You can most certainly combine these two decks together and enhance the readings that you get. The Healing Codes will provide you with a more complete picture and increase the energy in each one of the seven portals/chakras. You can also use any of these cards as portal/chakra Healing Activators. I have also included some wonderful Activator Grids in this guidebook to work with the energies of the Healing Codes even further.

Here is a quick at-a-glance list of the energies and extra guidance for interpreting and working with the Healing Codes:

HEALING CODES:

30. Success, 396 Hz FREEDOM HEALING CODE
Stimulates courage, groundedness, and the sense of triumph over obstacles
Associated with the ROOT PORTAL

4. Acceleration, 417 Hz CLEANSING HEALING CODE
Shifts negative or self-sabotaging subconscious programming and inspires creativity
Associated with the SACRAL PORTAL

35. Repair, 528 Hz MIRACLES HEALING CODE
Initiates DNA repair and transformation and promotes empowerment
Associated with the SOLAR PORTAL

15. Compassion, 639 Hz LOVE HEALING CODE
Inspires gravitation toward high frequencies of love, compassion, and harmony
Associated with the HEART PORTAL

12. Expansion, 741 Hz ENLIGHTEN HEALING CODE
Supports purification, clear communication, and assertiveness
Associated with the THROAT PORTAL

37. Metamorphosis, 852 Hz CLARITY HEALING CODE
Expands intuition, encourages mental peace, and inspires innovative solutions
Associated with the THIRD-EYE PORTAL

41. Unification, 963 Hz ONENESS HEALING CODE
Connects with the Divine Creator and ignites unity consciousness
Associated with the CROWN PORTAL

A Note about Reversals for Healing Codes

Since the Healing Codes exist to help you integrate the higher, more-refined vibrations and frequencies of purity, if your card reading displays any of these cards, **the focus is more on integration and upgrading frequencies,** rather than taking actions for rebalancing. However, if your card shows up in a reverse position, you could also alternatively read these in the same manner I described with the Healing Shields. Except in this case, **if the Healing Codes show a reversal, it might indicate that you may need to attend more closely to one or more of the chakra energies.** It may be indicating a need for some clearing before the upgrade can occur. Again, feel free to assign your own meanings to the Healing Codes on the basis of your inquiries, your intuition, and the scope of your reading.

The Angels, Ascended Masters, and Elementals

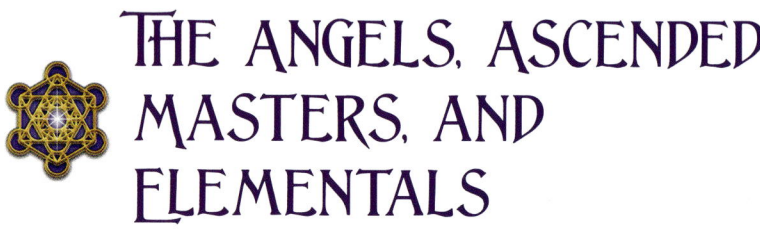

The remaining 18 cards in the *Celestial Frequencies* oracle deck are a combination of energies from the Elemental, Faerie, Ascended Masters, and otherworldly realms. These 18 cards are designated with the Metatron's Cube icon, which is linked with Archangel Metatron's energies. Archangel Metatron is an angelic guardian who has mastery over the flow of creation energies and provides a direct connection to the divine. He is also referred to as "the Voice of God." The energies of these 18 cards emanate a high voltage of light that encourages creativity, initiates divine guidance, and brings clarity for your card readings or Activator Healing Grids. They will all bring enhanced frequencies from their respective realms or vibrational content. All the colors that are connected to each image bring their own sense of support. The sacred color rays that were depicted in my *Magical Dimensions Oracle* still remain vibrant and alive in the *Celestial Frequencies* oracle deck as well, and you now have an even-wider variety of color rays for healing, activation, and inspiration.

NUMEROLOGY SIGNIFICANCE

In the bottom left-hand corner of each oracle card, you'll notice a number. Each card in the *Celestial Frequencies* and *Magical Dimensions* oracle decks are numbered and linked with the concepts of numerology. Numbers carry specific vibrations, and they can have a profound effect on our energies. The art images I've created for these special decks have been carefully selected and assigned with a specific number, which is encoded with numerological significance. This adds yet another dynamic layer of magic and celestial mystery to these special decks! You, as the oracle reader, can exercise your intuition and enhance your card readings by tapping into the artistry of the cards and their numerology connections.

    Even though I have not included a specific guide to the numbers and their relationships to my artwork, there is a definite synergy between them. However, I leave this discovery completely up to you to decipher their connections. Those who are familiar with numerology will be one step ahead! However, your interpretations will depend on if you are deferring to Pythagorean numerology or Egyptian gematria, and so on. For those unfamiliar with numerology, perhaps this is an invitation to delve more deeply into this topic. Meanwhile, to gain the most clarity from your card readings, simply use your intuition and focus simultaneously on the card numbers and the associated imagery. Listen closely to the numbers with your extrasensory perception and be open to receiving spontaneous insights about how the numbers relate to the images. Most importantly, have fun with your venture onward and forward into the inner mystical quest of numbers!

CLEANSING AND CARE OF YOUR NEW DECK
KEEPING IT CLEAN

Before consulting the *Celestial Frequencies* oracle deck for personal or client readings, please first cleanse your new deck. These cards are highly activational and will hold their high frequencies; however, due to the product being printed, packaged, and shipped by outside vendors and so on, you'll want to cleanse the energies of all the previous handlers of the package.

To cleanse the deck after you open the package, you can use a variety of methods, depending on what resonates with you best. Some suggested methods include the following:

- *Burn sage, palo santo, cedarwood, lavender flowers, sweetgrass, mugwort, or other clarifying incense and allow the smoke to permeate all sides of the cards.*
- *Rub lavender, sage, eucalyptus, or lemon essential oil between your hands, allow it to absorb, and then lightly wave your hands over the cards. (You can also use an essential oil diffuser or air spray, as long as you don't get the cards wet.)*
- *Use a cleansed quartz crystal or Herkimer diamond and set it on top of the deck for a few minutes.*
- *Use sound to cleanse the deck, with either a toning bell, Tibetan tingsha, or rain stick around the entire deck.*
- *Use your own voice to cleanse the deck with a single Om or voice tone of your choice. (This deck is particularly attuned to sound healing frequencies and would LOVE a sound healing bath every now and again!)*
- *Gently blow on the deck with your breath of life!*
- *Place your deck overnight in fresh bay leaves, or on a bed of fresh flower petals*

SPECIAL HIGH-FREQUENCY CLEANSING SYMBOL

There is a special high-frequency light code symbol printed on the inside of the box. **This sacred symbol serves to keep the cards energetically clean while they are stored in the box,** so it is recommended to store your cards back in the box after doing a reading for yourself or others. That way, your deck will always remain clear at all times. If you are using any of the cards as Healing Activator Grids, it is a good idea to at least place the cards back into the box for a few minutes before and after your grids so you will be ensured of clear frequencies prior and after use.

This symbol continually circulates a highly potent light resonance field that is attuned with The Creator's loving divine frequencies. The symbol will always remain pure and clear, so that whatever you place in the box will also be cleansed and match to the level of these higher frequencies.

You may, by all means, choose to use your own box, velvet bag, or other storage device for keeping your cards clean while not in use. The symbol in the box is just an extra bonus so you won't have to continually keep cleansing your cards. Although it is a good practice to cleanse the cards after each use, if kept in the box with the cleansing symbol, your deck will remain fresh and cleared of obstructive energies.

I realize that many readers like to cleanse their oracle decks in their own unique ways, so please feel free to experiment with your own types of cleansing.

Establishing a Connection and Your Focus

Now that your new deck is cleared, cleansed, vibrationally purified, and ready to go, you can infuse and set your own personal focus for the use of your cards. You can recite a private prayer over the deck to call upon your Higher Self, Angels, Spiritual Guides, Ascended Masters, Elementals, and Galactic Family, or a direct prayer to Creator Source/God, or whatever feels right to you—**just as long as you state that these cards be used for the highest good of all, and that they always continue to be infused with love, light, God, and truth.** This covers most everything and keeps frequencies in the light and aligned with the highest vibrations of love at all times.

A note about connecting with Angels, Elementals, Galactics, or Ascended Masters. When working with these cards and calling on the assistance of any of these beings residing in the various dimensions, **please always ask to be connected with the highest echelons of love before engaging in communications.** Just as there are many beautiful and loving souls that wish to assist you, there are also fragmented energies that engage in lower vibrational activities. Please refrain from obtaining guidance from these nonhelpful entities.

Always clear your own energies, surround yourself with white and liquid golden light, and do your own blessing or meditation before beginning communication with these cards. You can also shuffle the cards while setting your intentions, since this will further refine and focus your energies.

Holding the deck in your hands and reciting the following affirmation statement out loud is but one example of how to connect with this deck: *"I attune my intuition with the highest frequencies of this oracle deck aligned with the energies of clarity, truth, love, and grace. May all the messages, insights, healing, and activation I receive from this deck for myself and others be highly accurate, clear, and empowering."*

Alternatively, you can recite this same affirmation statement and insert a very specific focus in place, if you desire a specific usage of the deck before a reading. For example: *"I attune my intuition with the highest frequencies of this oracle deck aligned with the energies of clarity, truth, love, and grace. I place my focus on receiving guidance for (and then state your purpose here . . . such as gaining advice on your career, relationships, spirituality, health, life purpose, or whatever specific input you'd like). May all the messages, insights, healing, and activation I receive with this deck for myself and others be highly accurate, clear, and empowering."*

Another great way to connect with each card is to touch or tap each individual card with your fingers to tell the cards you are ready for expansion and transformation. Or you can simply knock on the back of the deck three times to signal that you are ready for the reading.

IMPORTANT NOTE: I highly recommend spending some time to sift through your cards one at a time prior to use, so that you can connect with each of the energies separately. You'll want to carefully separate all the cards anyway, since when you first receive your deck, the cards tend to stick together due to the printing process. So, please take some time and gently separate them one by one so they will be easier to shuffle.

Obtaining Guidance From Your Deck
Clarity Before Answers

This deck was created to help strengthen your intuitive and psychic abilities, initiate self-healing, and assist you in receiving guidance from cosmic and celestial energies. The suggested card spreads can be used for personal readings or professional client sessions. They are meant to provide a starting point. These spreads are nontraditional, and they will provide profound insights for your inquiries.

When it comes time to obtaining guidance from your *Celestial Frequencies* oracle deck, it will be helpful to first postulate your question with clarity. The energies of this deck are unique, and they link to celestial vibrations and Divine Light Codes, so it is best to center yourself in a higher-perspective mindset before making your inquiries. This will greatly assist in ensuring you are open to receiving the best interpretations, either for yourself or your clients.

There are a few ways to phrase your inquiries for this deck. You could ask the cards a question—something simple, such as *"What do I need to know right now?"*—the cards will give you a general overview in this case, but that may not provide you with a lot of detail. However, obtaining an overview of your situation may be exactly what you need, if you merely want to know whatever is coming up for you in that moment. In these instances, just fine-tune your intuition to interpret which area of your life the cards are referring to. Alternatively, if you ask, *"What do I need to know right now that can help me improve communications with my partner, John?,"* you'll receive a bit more clarity in that specific area of inquiry. Sometimes an overview is all that is needed; other times, you'll want a more specific message. Just be clear on the front end if you want an overview or more details, and feel free to pick additional cards if you need more clarification on your reading.

The energies of these cards will amplify your state of being, mostly because the frequencies that emanate from this deck have a tendency to inspire you to step forward into a higher octave of your own light. The artwork in this deck was created in a high vibrational state, so naturally the energy will remain in those higher bandwidths of frequencies. It will be up to you to raise your own frequencies to match that of the deck's high light of clarity. This doesn't mean you have to be perfect; otherwise, why else would you be consulting the cards, right? Just keep in mind that if you're unclear on your initial inquiry, or if you consult the cards with blocked energies, you might also receive an unclear message. If the guidance you receive seems unclear or fuzzy, just rephrase your question and continue onward, or choose a few extra cards to clarify the initial reading.

Remember, you hold the keys to your clarity and ultimate happiness. My goals are always to serve and empower you to make your own decisions on the basis of what feels best and right for you. But with these cards, you now have some additional tools to help you view your situations from higher perspectives.

Most importantly, never ever let anyone take your power away. Period. Always trust yourself and your intuition. You are truly the master of your own destiny, and you are responsible for your own choices. My oracle decks are merely tools to assist you with receiving spiritual guidance, but ultimately you always have free will. It is important that you make choices and decisions that feel in alignment and resonant with your own internal guidance.

Unique Oracle Card Spreads

You are about to engage in a time of discovery, an inward journey that will activate your life, ignite your psychic and intuitive abilities, and link you with the cosmic realms. The energies of these cards are powerful, potent, and inspiring, and the frequencies of the images will work with you or your clients even beyond the completion of your oracle-reading sessions.

WILDSTAR MYSTIC SPREAD
(Clarity on Any Topic)

Let your starry-eyed intuition run wild! With the **Wildstar Mystic Spread**, you can pick any number of cards and place them in any manner of your choosing. Remember to focus and get clarity first, then phrase your inquiry appropriately while shuffling the deck. Listen to your inner guidance to choose the number of cards that you are drawn to, and lay out them before you. Use your intuition to guide you with assigning unique meanings to each card placement. Allow your own interpretations to emerge as you meditate upon what is being revealed. Trust whatever interpretation you receive, or if you need further guidance or clarity on the reading, pick another card or two for more insights.

ZERO-POINT BALANCER SPREAD
(Singular Overview to Rebalance a Situation)

```
┌─────────────────┐
│                 │
│                 │
│   CODE 1        │
│                 │
│   ZERO          │
│                 │
│   POINT         │
│                 │
│   BALANCER      │
│                 │
│                 │
└─────────────────┘
```

Reclaim your inner feng shui. The **Zero-Point Balancer** singular overview reading will be best suited for inquiries when your situation feels out of balance. The reading will provide insights for the most relevant energy in that particular moment for which you are doing the reading. The emphasis of this spread is on what can assist you (or your client) in returning back to a state of balance, the zero-point grounded place. A good example question for this reading would be *"What is most important for me to focus on right now in order to bring this situation back into balance?"*

Shuffle the deck while asking your question. Then spread the cards before you, choose one card from the deck that you're most drawn to, and turn the card face up. **The chosen card (Code 1) will provide you with the most relevant insight into what can most greatly assist your situation at this moment.**

GAIAN ACTIVATION SPREAD
(Gaining Insights into Your Next Steps Forward)

```
┌─────────────────┐     ┌─────────────────┐
│                 │     │                 │
│     CODE 1      │     │     CODE 2      │
│                 │     │                 │
│     INITIAL     │     │      NEXT       │
│                 │     │                 │
│      FIRST      │     │      STEP       │
│                 │     │                 │
│      STEP       │     │     FORWARD     │
│                 │     │                 │
└─────────────────┘     └─────────────────┘
```

The **Gaian Activation Spread** is a great reading for gaining insights into the best action steps that will assist you with your most important inquiry. This reading is for those who want practical and purposeful action steps to assist with either enhancing, transforming, or altering the progression of a situation.

I lovingly refer to Earth as "the Jewel of Terra," and this beautiful and precious jewel that we all reside on is a living, breathing being, named Gaia. Very simply, Gaia is life; the very soul and mother of Earth. She is the abundant and nurturing goddess who is steward of this planet, offering her nourishment to all of us. You will work hand in hand with Mother Gaia in this spread, where the focus is on getting down-to-earth guidance and insights. Who better to ask for assistance than from the Earth Mother herself!

As you shuffle the deck, a few good example questions for this reading would be *"What does Gaia wish to share with me about my next steps forward?"* or something like *"What specific actions can be the most helpful in this situation?"* The focus for this reading is on obtaining specific guidance that can either improve or shift the outcome. As you shuffle the cards, keep this as the focus of your inquiry and then intuitively choose two cards from the deck.

The first card chosen **(Code 1) is the first initial step that will be the most beneficial, and the second card chosen (Code 2) is the next step that will help foster a favorable outcome. Alternatively, if you prefer, you can read these two codes as one combined action step.** Begin this oracle reading with a two-card choice, and then if you need further guidance, feel free to pick additional cards.

COSMIC-LADDER SPREAD
(For Aligning with Successful Outcomes)

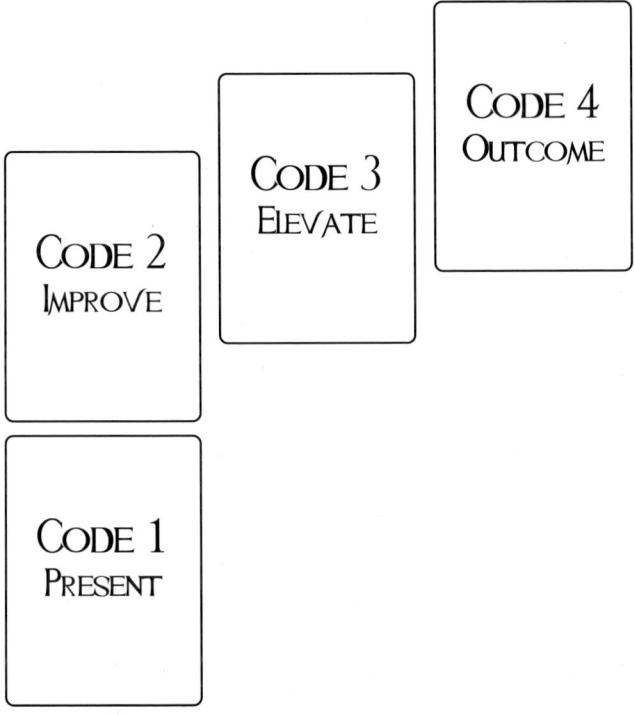

The **Cosmic-Ladder Spread** is another unique and fun spread to help you climb a cosmic ladder of ultimate success. Guidance can be gleaned from this reading on a range of topics: relationships, health, career, money, spiritual growth, or just about any other situation for which you wish to obtain intuitive guidance.

As you shuffle the deck, a few good example questions for this reading would be *"**What is most important for me to know that will improve my health condition?**"* or *"**How can I align my mindset with activating prosperity and abundance in my life?**"* The card placements will display the energies surrounding your inquiries, what can be improved, how to elevate the situation, and ultimately how to be successful in your endeavors. You can also use this reading to expand on the **Gaian Activation Spread**, except in the **Cosmic Ladder** it's all about exploring additional energies that can make your situation a total success. As you shuffle the cards, ask the deck to bring you more clarity on how to raise the entire situation to a higher frequency.

The chosen card **(Code 1)** is the **present** and shows you the energies surrounding your present situation—the now. *(Alternatively, you can use one, or both, of the cards you picked from the Gaian Activation Spread as a starting point for this reading.)*

The chosen card **(Code 2)** is the **improvement** that can be made, alluding to what changes or alterations will ensure the most grace and ease in your situation.

The chosen card **(Code 3)** is the **elevation** and provides insights into which energies are needed to raise this situation to a higher vibration.

The chosen card **(Code 4)** is the **outcome**, showing what is necessary for ultimate success and for the highest good for all involved.

Pyramid Builder Spread
(For Projects, Partnerships, and New Opportunities)

The **Pyramid Builder Spread** is geared toward establishing template and blueprint enhancements for projects, partnerships, and new opportunities. This spread provides insights into tools that can be put in place that can help strengthen the entire situation of your inquiry, and is ideally suited for questions about specific projects (either personal or career related).

As you shuffle the deck, some good example questions for this reading would be *"What is most important for me to know about the logistics of my new educational business venture?"* or *"How will this partnership with Shane assist my current creative project?"* This reading provides you with the appropriate foundation, substance, and alignment that need to be established in order to provide the best outcome for your projects. This spread is also very helpful for providing insights in relation to new opportunities that may come across your path. The card placements will show you the energies surrounding your project or opportunity and will initiate new insight for which blueprints and tools are needed to build your new or existing project with a strong, solid, and grounded beginning.

(Codes 1–3 are considered the foundation cards in this reading. The stability of the pyramid.)

The chosen card **(Code 1)** depicts the **beginning** energies of the current project/opportunity and its surrounding energy.

The chosen card **(Code 2)** relays the **existing terrain** and shows the current energies of how you are personally relating to the project or opportunity. Your assessment of the situation.

The chosen card **(Code 3)** displays the **foundational grounding,** bringing forth insights into how to best stabilize the project or opportunity so it feels more grounded.

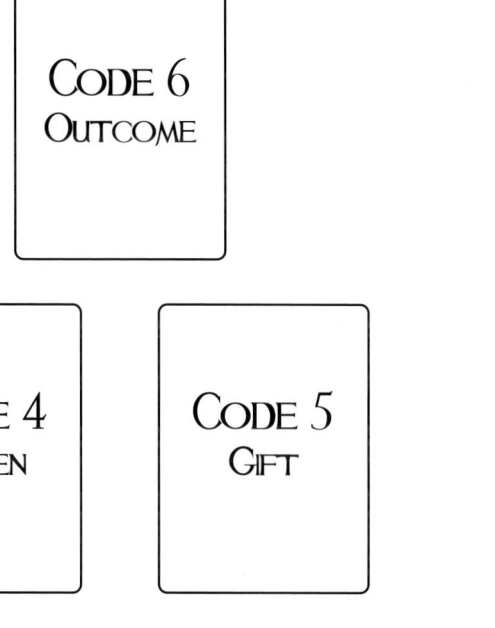

(Codes 4–5 are considered the substance cards in this reading. The central core of the pyramid.)

The chosen card **(Code 4)** exposes the **hidden influence or obstacle,** the unconscious of what needs to be exposed that is not being spoken about.

The chosen card **(Code 5)** displays the **gift of transformation** when you acknowledge the obstacle and make necessary adjustments. This ensures that the entire landscape shifts so the situation moves toward the most desirable outcome.

(Code 6 is considered the final harmonic alignment in this reading. The apex of the pyramid.)

The chosen card **(Code 6)** represents the **ultimate outcome** after integration of all the other cards.

UNIQUE ORACLE CARD SPREADS

COURSE CORRECTION SPREAD
(For Life Path, Purpose, Mission Alignment)

The **Course Correction Spread** is ideal for questions surrounding life path, purpose, and mission and discovering if you are headed in the right direction. With this spread, you'll learn the trajectory of your current path and identify if you need any course correction along the way. Normally, I do not recommend making inquiries that would prompt only a "yes" or "no" response from the cards. However, for this particular spread, this is precisely what we want when we get to the middle section of the reading at Code 4.

As you shuffle the deck, a few good example questions for this type of reading would be *"Am I currently on a career path for my highest and best good?"* or *"Does my relationship with Emily need to shift in a different direction?"* This line of questioning will prompt the trajectory card **(Code 4)** to be the signal of a "yes" or "no" when you need to know if you should pick additional cards for the reading.

The chosen card **(Code 1)** depicts your **current** inquiry and its surrounding emotion and energy.

The chosen card **(Code 2)** relays your **past,** and shadows the energies of your past consciousness in relation to your current inquiry.

The chosen card **(Code 3)** illuminates the **lesson(s),** the growth and wisdom pathways for you to attain while on this current path.

The chosen card **(Code 4)** is the **trajectory** of your current path and foreshadows the surrounding energies of what may be to come if you remain in your current situation. This card emphasizes a possible turning point, a smoke signal to your intuition should you desire to pick more cards for this reading. If the trajectory card is a desirable one, or if you feel confident with the chosen cards **(Codes 1–3)** in your reading thus far, then the reading stops here. However, if the trajectory card shows a less-than-desirable outcome, then you may wish to *course-correct* and choose another set of cards. In that case, pick three new cards, which should be sufficient to provide more information about your inquiry, to learn what will be in store for the new decisions based on your new alignment.

(Codes 5–7 represent the **new course correction**, only if you felt you needed to continue onward.)

The chosen card **(Code 5)** displays the **new energies** that will arise once you make your trajectory shift or choice to move in a different direction.

The chosen card **(Code 6)** provides the **challenges or opportunities** that you may encounter with the new pathway ahead.

The chosen card **(Code 7)** is the **outcome** and the energies that surround your decision, if and when you make choices to switch gears.

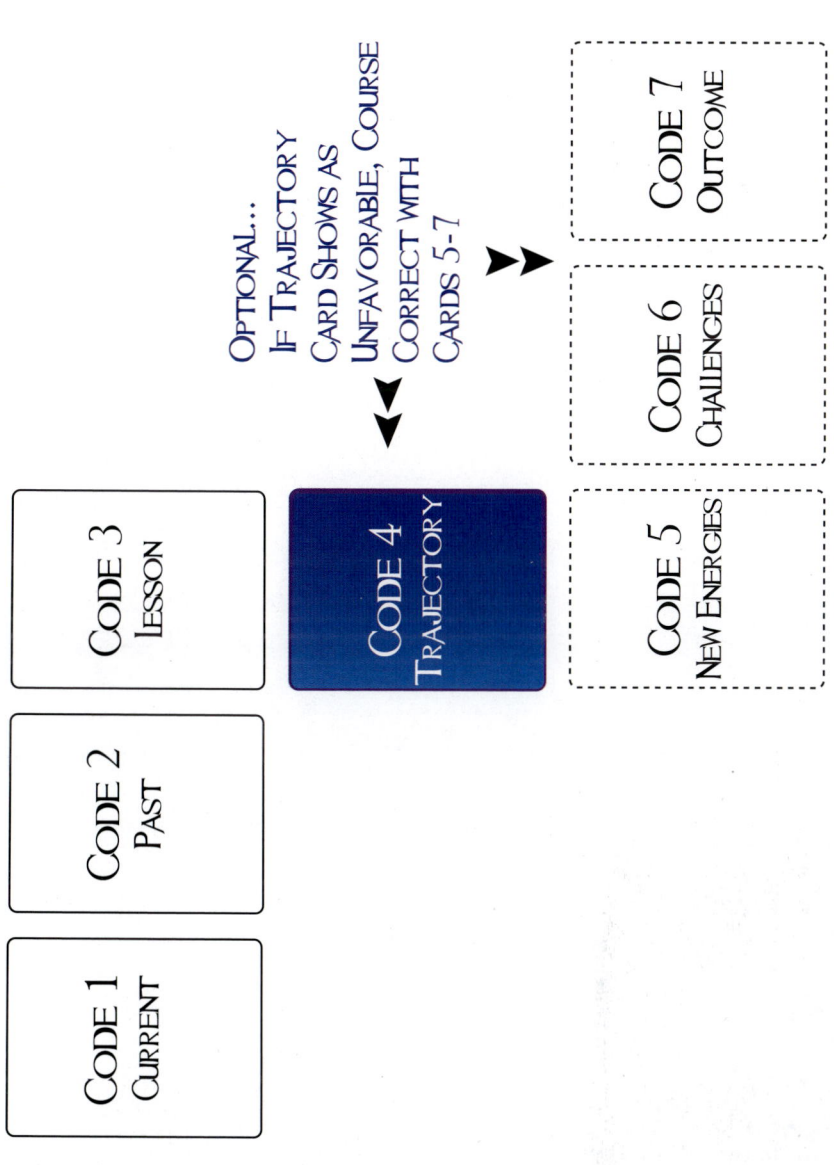

Celestial-Timeline-Sequencing Spread
(Provides Clarity for Different Timelines)

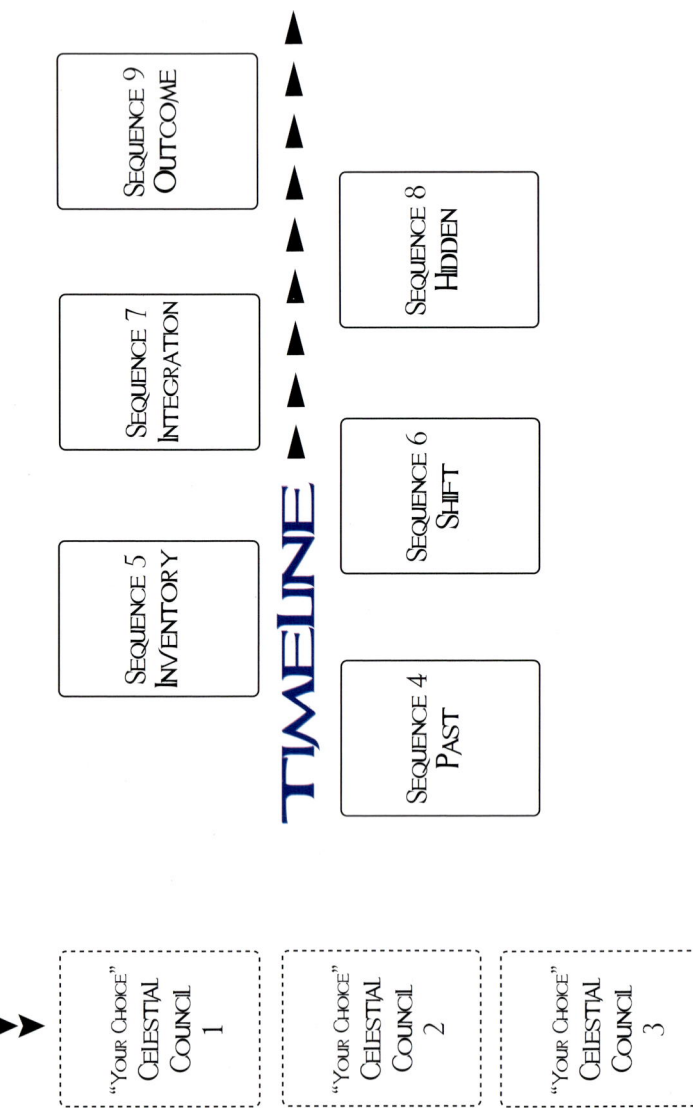

The **Celestial-Timeline-Sequencing Spread** is unique in that it specifically dials into cosmic frequencies, where you'll receive direct guidance from the galactic and multidimensional energies that are infused into this deck. The first thing you'll want to do is extract all 12 of the cards in this deck that are considered the "Master Galactic Energies." The following list provides the card numbers for these 12 cards, and the galactic races these cards are associated with:

3. Inspiration (Cassiopeia)
8. Sovereignty (Orion)
10. Decisiveness (Sirius)
11. Love (Pleiades)
13. Discernment (Vega)
20. Resilience (Lyra)
22. Focused (The Guardians, a blending of various galactic races)
24. Magnetism (Telos)
25. Innovative (Andromeda)
27. Curiosity (Zeta)
36. Infinite (Arcturus)
42. Collaboration (The Alliance, a collaborative group of multidimensional cosmic beings)

Once you've separated these 12 cards from the deck, choose three cards from these 12 to which you are most drawn and intuitively resonate with the strongest in this moment, then set them aside. These three chosen cards now serve as your celestial council members for this reading. Return and reshuffle the remaining nine cards back into the main deck.

Spread these three cards, your celestial council members, out in front of you (either horizontally or vertically, or however you wish). Pose your questions directly to them. Since this reading is focused on timelines, as you shuffle the deck a couple of good practical example questions would be *"What will be the most appropriate timeline to leave my current job?"* or *"What is the best timeline for my relocation to England?"* However, you can also ask your celestial council higher-dimensional questions such as *"What do you have in store for my next spiritual upgrade?"* or *"How can I best prepare before my next spiritual teacher arrives?"*

Now that you have set the stage for your celestial council, you can begin with your timeline-sequencing spread with card placement **(Sequence 4)**. The placements in this spread will highlight the energies surrounding your question, and the sequencing shows in order of the timeline.

(Celestial Council Cards 1, 2, 3 represents your **specific galactic council members** who are most attuned with addressing your questions.)

The chosen card **(Sequence 4)** reflects the **past** sequence, which shows where you've been in the energies of past patterns with your inquiry.

The chosen card **(Sequence 5)** displays taking **inventory** on what you have gained up to this point and the lessons you have learned from the past.

The chosen card **(Sequence 6)** provides **the shift** and highlights what is needed to change, transform, or release in order to move forward into the most favorable timeline.

The chosen card **(Sequence 7)** marks the **integration** of what needs to be unified and strengthened after shifts are made.

The chosen card **(Sequence 8)** exposes the **hidden elements** of what is unconscious and needs to be exposed or unveiled and brought forth into awareness.

The chosen card **(Sequence 9)** displays the destination, the **final outcome,** which shows the future destiny with this entire reading and what changes are necessary to fully implement the sequence and timeline of this inquiry.

CREATION SPIRAL SPREAD
(INSIGHTS FOR CREATING AND DETAILING STEPS FORWARD)

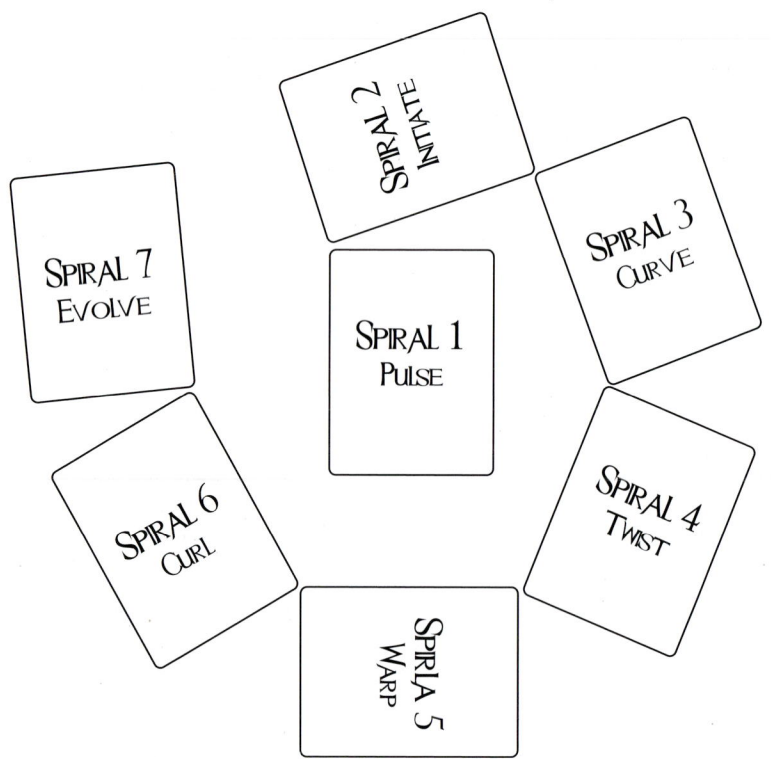

The **Creation Spiral Spread** helps you navigate through a magnetizing array of creation energies for gaining insights. The cards you choose will create a momentum of spiral energy that will provide further details for each step forward. Your journey begins with a question such as *"What is important for me to know about the blockages I am experiencing with creating my ideal career?"* or *"What steps can I take to magnetize a soulmate partnership into my life?"* The formation begins with a pulse, but with each radiating arm of light it builds into a spiral energy of creation. Once you attain the first spiral insight, move to the next spiral, integrate, and keep progressing forward. As you integrate each insight, your situation becomes increasingly clearer, and you fuse more in alignment with the spiral . . . until you feel unity with the undeniable fact that you are the ultimate creator of your own reality.

The chosen card **(Spiral 1)** is the **pulse** of the creation spiral and relays the energy surrounding the entire issue.

The chosen card **(Spiral 2)** is the **initiation** point that ignites your second code, providing the overall energy of what is being created. Your starting point.

The chosen card **(Spiral 3)** begins the **curve**, signifying the direction of where your creation is going.

The chosen card **(Spiral 4)** displays the **twist**, which highlights any changes that need to be made in order to adjust the curve.

The chosen card **(Spiral 5)** is where the **warp** phase comes in, showing the pitfalls to become aware of once you make any adjustments.

The chosen card **(Spiral 6)** begins the **curl**, which energetically shows the level of supportive frequencies you will encounter along this journey of creation.

The chosen card **(Spiral 7)** is the **evolution** phase, which completes the spiral energy up to this point. If you follow this Creation Spiral, it will take all the previous spiral cards into account and foreshadows the outcome of what will be created.

Feel free to intuitively choose additional cards if you would like to continue the spiral vortex even further.

Healing Activator Grids

In addition to using the *Celestial Frequencies* oracle deck for daily oracle readings, these cards can also be utilized as what I call "Healing Activator Grids" for either personal or client use. In this section you'll learn how to use the cards in this manner. Included are some sample Healing Grids to begin your Activator journey.

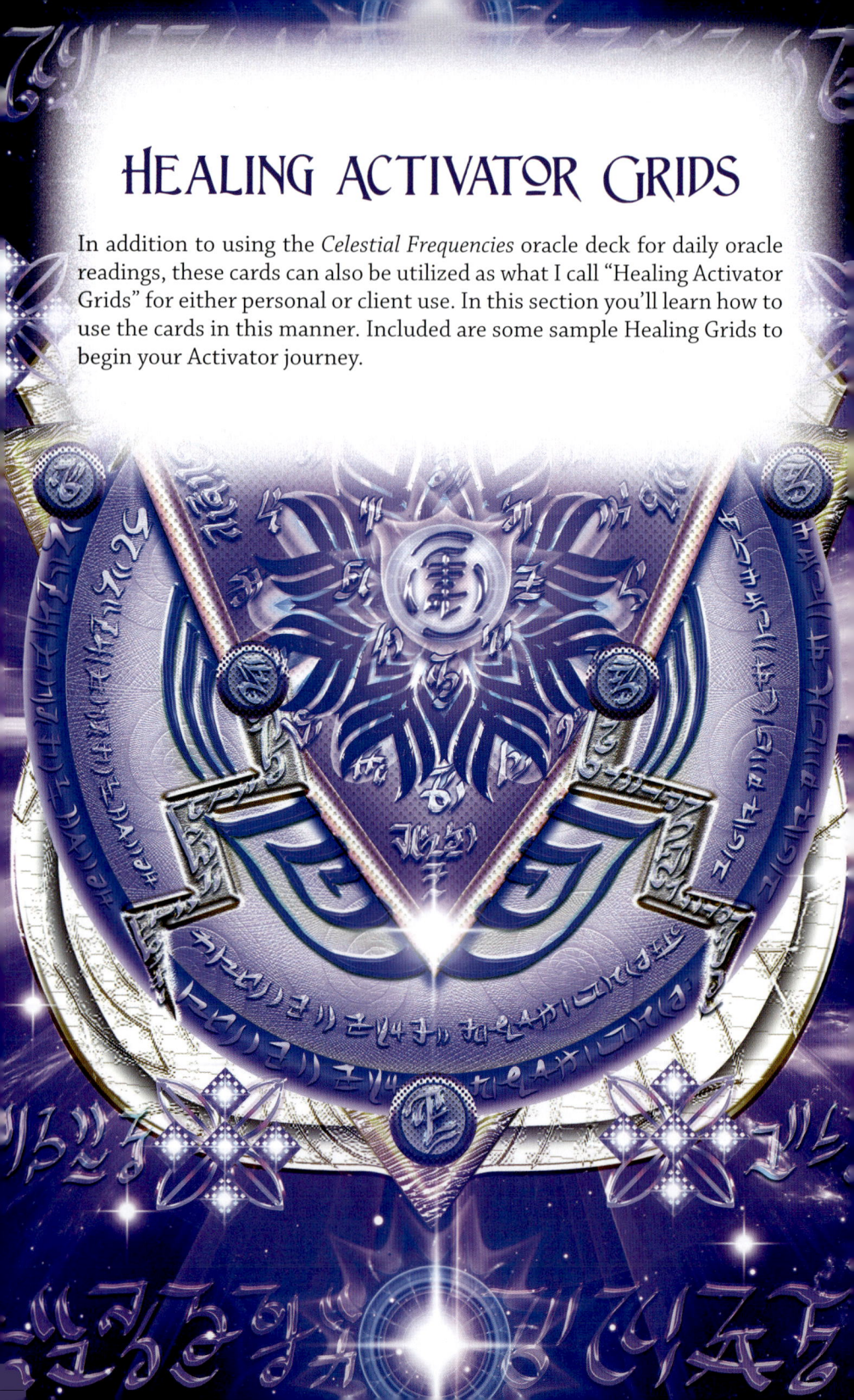

There are really unlimited uses for these Healing Activators, and the more you utilize this deck, the more you'll develop your own ways to further expand their energies as time goes on. You can utilize any of the cards in this deck to create your own unique Healing Activator Grids. Initiate your intuitive guidance and choose the cards that most call to you. Although if you need a starting point, I do provide suggestions for more-detailed and more-specific Healing Activator Grids below in the next few sections. I'm including a starter list of ideas and suggestions for their various applications:

- **Create a Healing Activator Grid with the cards on a table and work with the energies daily.**
- **Choose a card that you're drawn to and meditate with it in your hands to feel the energetic codes of the card enhancing your own bioenergetic field.**
- **Choose one or more of the 12 Master Galactic Energies of the deck and ask them to provide you with an energetic upgrade.**
- **Choose a card that you're drawn to, and place it under your pillow at night.**
- **Place a clear glass or organite coaster over the top of a chosen card and then set your water or liquid in a glass on top of the card to infuse the fluid with light frequencies. Then drink the liquid for a refreshing treat. Organite is a mixture of fiberglass resin, which can contain metallic shavings, crystals, or particles or powders that attract energy. It draws in negative energies and transmutes them into positive energy. Organite can work in tandem with these cards as an energy transmutation and generator device, depending on your focus of the specific Healing Activator Grids you are working with.**
- **Place a particular card on your bathroom mirror as a daily affirmation.**
- **Place a card of your choice in the console of your car to activate you as you drive.**
- **Place crystals on top of a chosen card to activate, cleanse, or infuse them with specific frequencies.**
- **Place necklaces, rings, or any jewelry item on a chosen card to clear, infuse, and recharge your jewelry pieces.**
- **Remove the seven Healing Code cards from the deck and place them on the floor underneath your massage table, or tape them to the underside of the table in alignment with the chakras system for a healing infusion.**
- **Remove the seven Healing Code cards from the deck and place them in or around crystal bowls and activate them even more by toning (they LOVE music and sound activation).**

- Remove the seven Healing Shield cards from the deck and place them by your bedside or nightstand to provide shielding while you sleep. When you awaken in the morning, use the seven Healing Shields to put on your full armor of frequency shielding.
- Energize and infuse your nutritional supplements by placing them on top of chosen cards.
- and so much more . . .

WORKING WITH THE HEALING ACTIVATOR GRIDS

The process of cleansing and setting your focus when using the Healing Activator Grids is the same process as for oracle cards. Proceed as mentioned earlier in this guidebook. The only difference is that when you set your focus for these Activator Grids, **just intend for them to be used for the purpose of whatever your chosen application (e.g., cleansing your crystals, energizing your water, working with the specific Healing Activator Grids, etc.).**

HAVE PATIENCE

These cards are aligned with very powerful frequencies of light and Divine Light Codes, so they will help you in shifting your bioenergetics toward these higher energies. The cards will become attuned to your unique process of receiving energy so that shifts and transformations go at your own pace. Sometimes shifts happen very rapidly; other times, it takes a bit more linear time. *So, please be patient with your own process.*

USING HEALING ACTIVATOR GRIDS WITH CLIENTS

Using the Healing Activator Grids for client sessions is different from the oracle readings. You are providing a tool to inspire your clients' activations to occur. To start off, use the suggested Healing Activator Grids provided in this guidebook, but you'll soon be intuitively creating your own grids based on your clients' unique concerns. To create a custom client Healing

Activator Grid, choose some starter cards from the deck that feel aligned with your client's current issue. Map out the cards in a visual grid that feels resonant with assisting them with that concern, and allow your clients to further customize and choose their own cards or other items to add to the Activator Grid.

If you wish to utilize this deck both for Healing Activators *and* daily oracle readings, I highly recommend that you invest in purchasing a second *Celestial Frequencies* oracle deck. That way, you can have one deck specifically designated for your regular oracle readings, and the other deck can be designated for Healing Activator Grids. Sometimes you might receive intuition that your Healing Activator Grid needs to be on an altar or table for days, weeks, or even months at a time, and then you won't have to keep removing each Healing Activator Grid in order to do your oracle readings. Alternatively, you can purchase the *Magical Dimensions* oracle deck and utilize those cards as your Activators. There are additional Activator layouts included in that deck's guidebook as well.

HEALING ACTIVATOR GRID SUGGESTIONS

The Healing Activator Grids can address a plethora of challenges and concerns that people might experience regularly in a number of areas: **relationships, creative projects, career, clearing negativity, magnetizing abundance**, and more. However, these Healing Activator Grids *amplify* positive energies as well, so they have a dual purpose. Start off with one Healing Grid that resonates with you the most. You'll then develop your own unique grid activations as your relationship with the cards grows, and the cards become more aligned with your energy. Have fun with it and use your intuition to guide you in creating super-fun grids that look beautiful as well as radiate positivity!

Pillars-of-Light Healing Activator Grid

The **Pillars-of-Light Healing Activator Grid** is a 10-card Activator. It is very helpful for moving a situation that feels stuck forward through to completion, making transformational changes, and infusing higher frequencies into the issue. This Healing Activator Grid is very powerful and can promote significant breakthroughs in whatever is sent through its healing gateway. It is beneficial for utilization in all types of situations: projects, relationship concerns, career questions, geographical locations, health challenges, and even clearing old patterns and negative energies. Basically, this is your one-stop-shop activator and can provide beneficial vibrations to help you breeze through your situation with more grace and ease.

The eight cards in this grid correspond to specified cards in this deck, and two of the cards are called "wildcards." Where you see the two card placements designated as **"Your Choice,"** this indicates an action step for you to intuitively scan the deck for other card frequencies that you wish to add to your Pillars-of-Light Healing Activator Grid. For the card placement in the center of the pillars, you can either choose one of the other cards in the deck or feel free to use a photograph or something else that symbolizes what you wish to activate. Once you have chosen your wildcard or other item, overlay them directly in the center section of the Pillars of Light.

It is important that the cards are placed so each card is touching at least one of the other cards, so the energy keeps consistent and flowing, with the exception of the "Your Choice" card in the middle of the gateway. This card does not need to be touching the other cards.

You can also overlay specific crystals, *white or purple candles*, photos, amulets, coins, flowers, healing statues, or liquid in a glass container on top of the cards. White selenite, apophyllite, purple fluorite, or clear quartz would all be great suggested crystals for this Activator Grid. Place your Pillar-of-Light Healing Activator Grid on an altar or table where you can energize it daily. Use the layout for however long you feel is beneficial. When you feel the energy is complete, just remove and cleanse the cards and begin your next Healing Activator Grid.

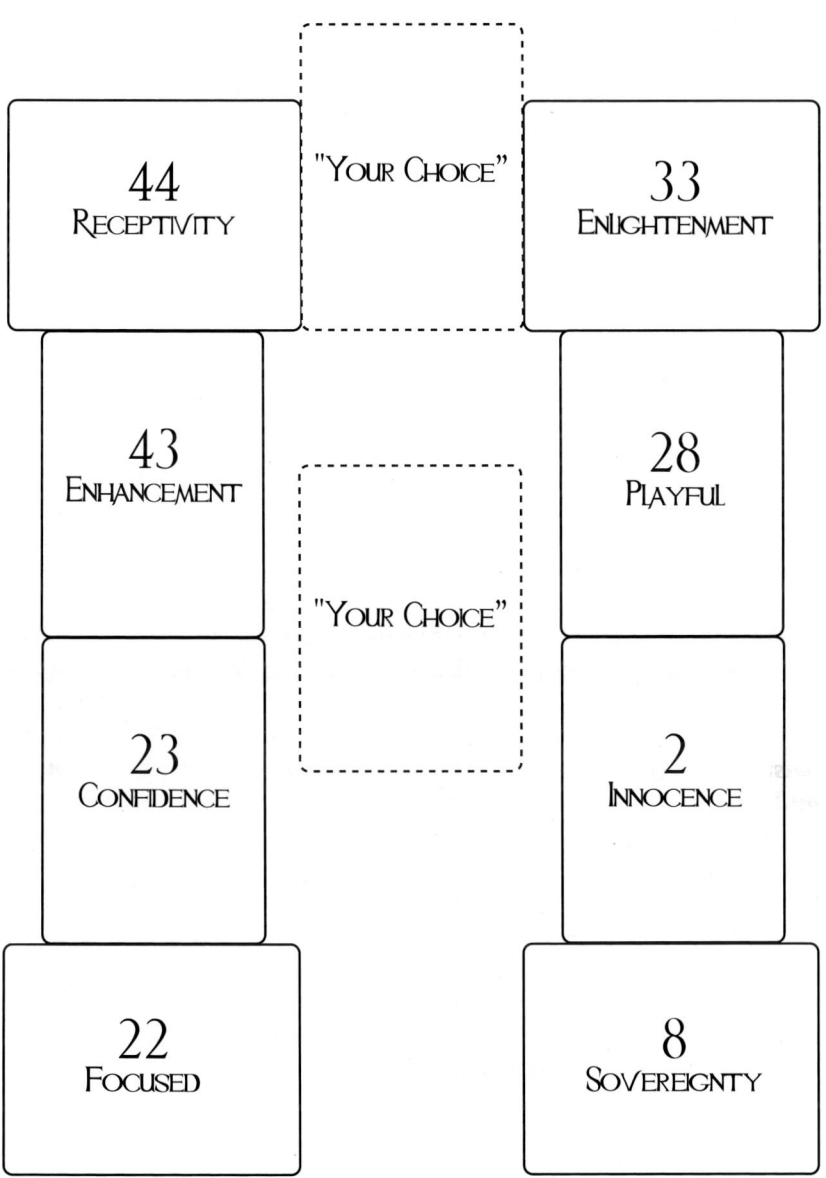

HEALING ACTIVATOR GRIDS

The Diamond Healing Activator Grid

The **Diamond Healing Activator Grid** is an 11-card Activator that is particularly helpful for clearing negativity and lower vibrations from any situation. You can also use this Healing Activator Grid for upgrading—reprogramming or deprogramming old patterns and transmuting them into positive frequencies. This Healing Activator Grid is very potent and can cleanse toxic energy from an entire room or can help dissolve triggers and charges that arise from challenging situations. There is no limitation on its use; however, this Activator Grid is particularly useful for clearing relationship imbalances, cleansing energy vampires, and dissolving negative emotions. If you utilize this Healing Activator Grid for cleansing and deprogramming, you can then engage this same Activator Grid for reprogramming—where you then infuse positive energy flow into that same situation.

The 10 card placements in this Activator correspond to the cards in this deck, except the 11th card placement is a wildcard designated as **"Your Choice"** and is meant for you to intuitively scan the deck for other frequencies that you wish to add to your Diamond Healing Activator Grid. You can either choose one card from the deck or feel free to use a photograph or something else that symbolizes what you wish to activate. Once you have chosen your wildcard or other item, overlay them directly on top and in the center section of the double-terminated diamond.

It is important that the cards are placed so each card is touching at least one of the other cards, so the energy keeps consistent and flowing, and the "Your Choice" card or item is set on the middle of the crystal grid.

You can also overlay specific crystals, *green or orange* candles, photos, amulets, coins, flowers, healing statues, or liquid in a glass container on top of the cards. Herkimer diamond, orange carnelian, double-terminated quartz, or aventurine all would be great suggested crystals for this grid. Place your Diamond Healing Activator Grid on an altar or table where you can energize it daily. Use the Healing Grid for however long you feel is beneficial. When you feel the energy is complete, just remove and cleanse the cards and begin your next Healing Activator Grid.

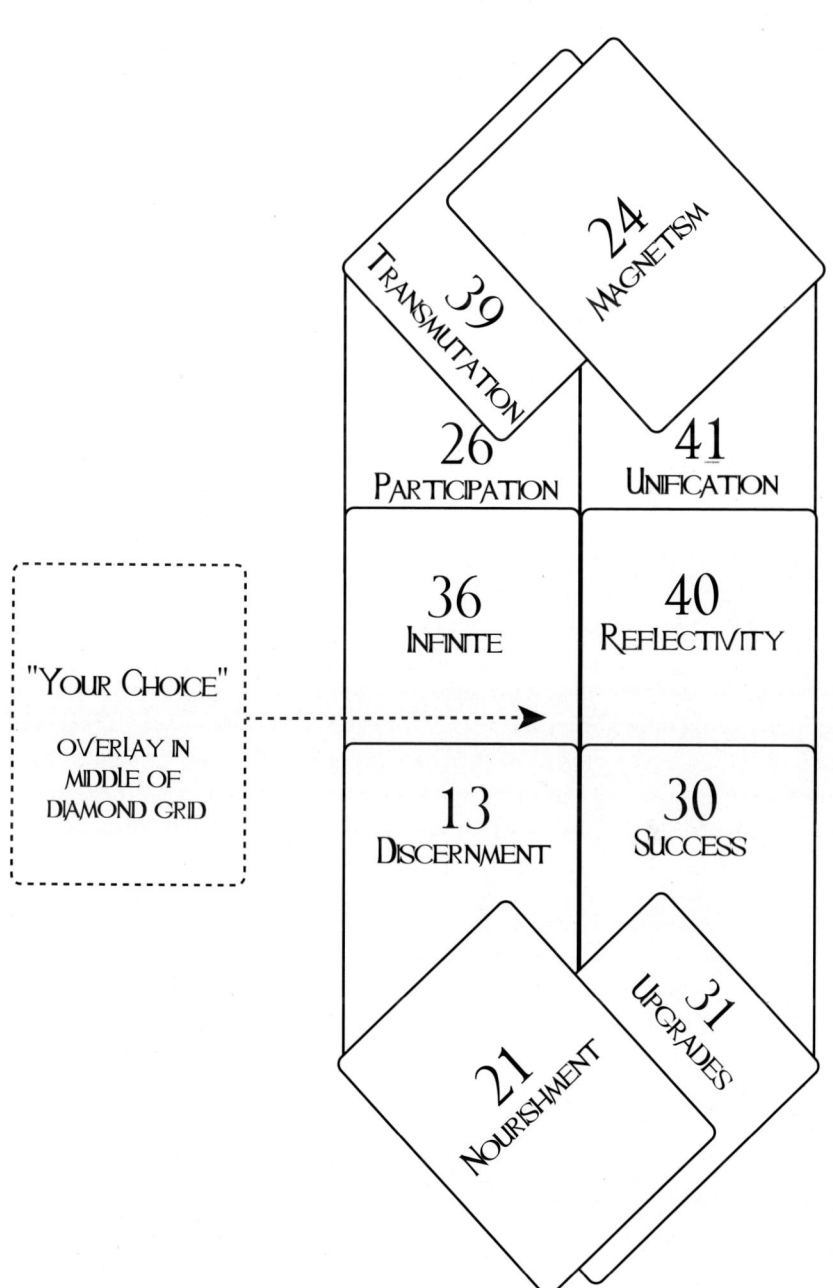

HEALING SHIELDS ACTIVATOR GRID

The **Healing Shields Activator Grid** is an 11-card Activator focused on obtaining shielding around your energy field from psychic attack, or when you need extra grounding and guardianship of your energy. This particular Activator utilizes all seven of the Healing Shields in the deck for the most comprehensive grounding. You will also be adding your own expression to this Healing Activator Grid. By utilizing all of the Healing Shields' energy forces, you will strengthen your own bioenergetic field—including your physical, spiritual, mental, and emotional bodies. You may experience some intensities with engaging this particular Activator Grid, since it is very empowering. You can also utilize this Activator Grid to surround a loved one with a shielding force of love, if they are experiencing heavy emotions of fear or anxiety.

The seven cards in this layout correspond to the cards in this deck, and four of them are "wildcards" designated as **"Your Choice"** and indicate for you to intuitively scan the deck for other frequencies that you wish to add to your Healing Shields Activator Grid. For the four "wildcard" placements at the top of the shield, you can either choose from the other cards in the deck or feel free to use photographs or something else that symbolizes what you wish to activate. Once you have chosen your wildcards or other items, overlay them in their proper placements in the Healing Shields Grid.

It is important that the cards are placed so each card is touching at least one of the other cards, so the energy keeps consistent and flowing. Ensure the "Your Choice" cards are also touching one another, if you decide to use your own photographs or other objects for these placements.

You can also overlay specific crystals, *red or blue* candles, photos, amulets, coins, flowers, healing statues, or liquid in a glass container on top of the cards. Black tourmaline, lapis, red jasper, or shungite all would be great suggested stones for this grid. Place your Healing Shields Activator Grid on an altar or table where you can energize it daily. Use the Activator Grid for however long you feel is beneficial. When you feel the energy is complete, just remove and cleanse the cards and begin your next Healing Activator Grid.

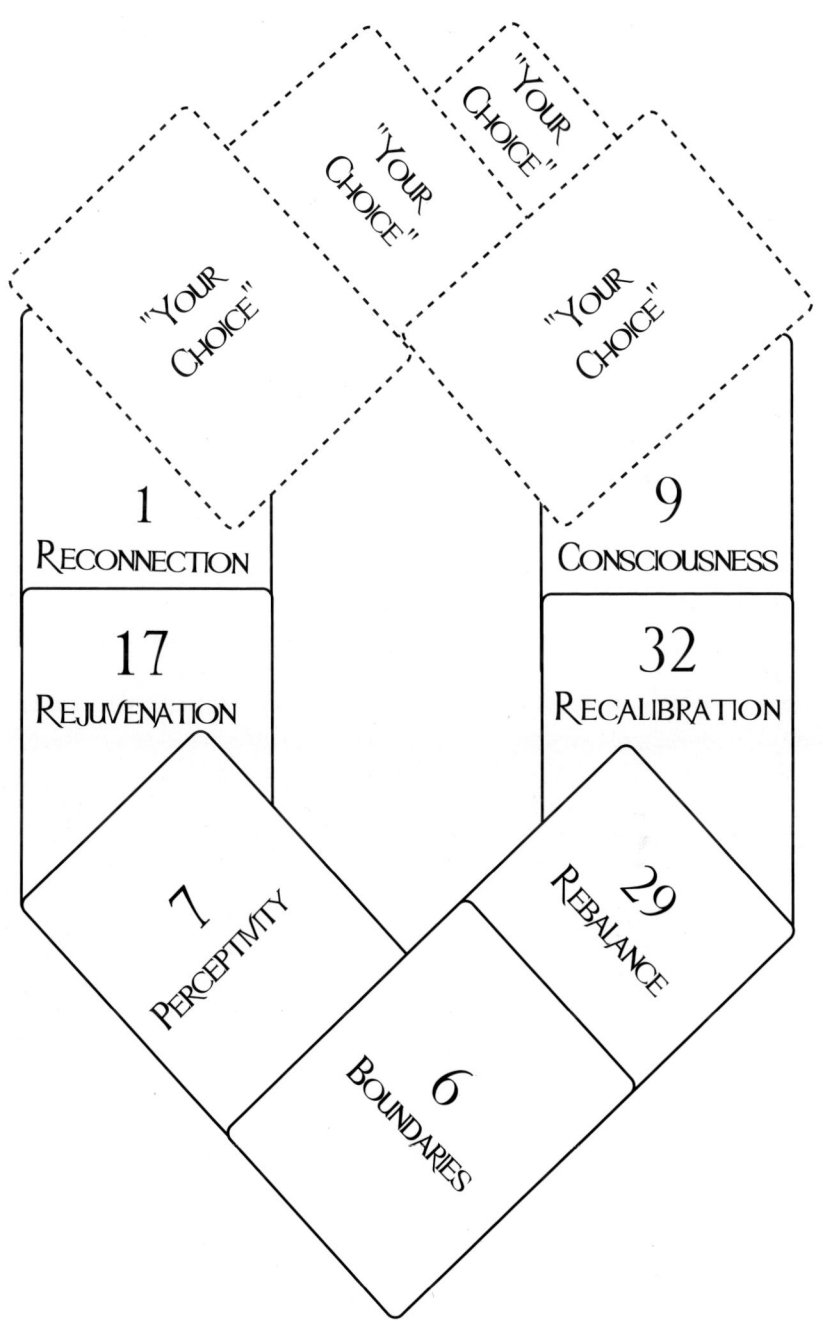

HEALING ACTIVATOR GRIDS 51

SONIC HARMONIZER HEALING ACTIVATOR GRID

The **Sonic Harmonizer Healing Activator Grid** is an 11-card Activator that initiates direct streams of high-frequency sound waves and will infuse pure and clean vibrations into whatever you wish to activate, since it utilizes all seven of the Healing Codes in this deck for enhancement and amplification. By including all the Healing Codes (which are linked with seven main Solfeggio frequency tones), you'll raise this Healing Activator Grid to a higher octave. These frequencies are extremely pure, and yet very strong at the same time, so you may experience a quickening in your energy field when working with the Sonic Harmonizer Grid.

There are seven cards in this layout that correspond to cards in the deck, and the remaining four cards are "wildcards," which are designated as **"Your Choice"** so you can intuitively scan the deck for other frequencies that you wish to add to your Sonic Harmonizer Grid. For the four-card placement at the endpoints of each of the two horizontal waves, you can either choose from the other cards in the deck or feel free to use photographs or something else that symbolizes what you wish to activate. By placing your own energetic choices in these endpoints of the grid, it prompts the main core of the Healing Codes to radiate pure tones from the center of the Activator and then connect with your own frequencies to energize, upgrade, and amplify them further.

It is important that the cards are placed so each card is touching at least one of the other cards, so the energy keeps consistent and flowing, so make sure that "Your Choice" cards at the endpoints of the grid are connected and touching the Healing Codes.

You can also overlay specific crystals, *pink or gold* candles, photos, amulets, coins, flowers, healing statues, or liquid in a glass container on top of the cards. Kunzite, rose quartz, or golden healer quartz all would be great suggested stones for this Healing Activator. Place your Sonic Harmonizer Healing Activator Grid on an altar or table where you can energize it daily. Use the Activator Grid for however long you feel is beneficial. When you feel the energy is complete, just remove and cleanse the cards and begin your next Healing Activator Grid.

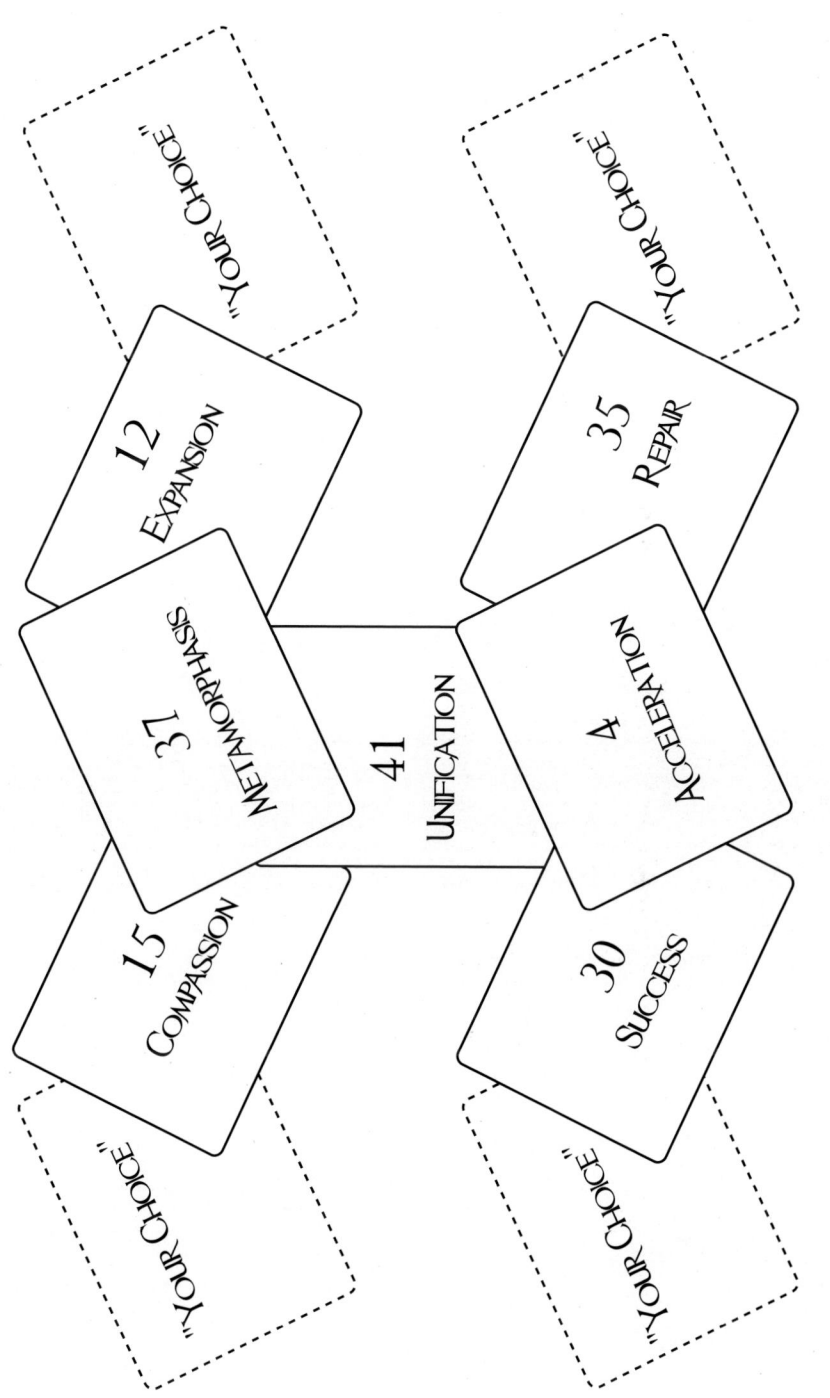

CELESTIAL FREQUENCIES 53

ORACLE CARD INTERPRETATIONS

RECONNECTION
Universal Healing Shield

 THE HEALING SHIELDS

1. RECONNECTION

To assist with reconnection and alignment with your Higher Self and directly to Creator Source
Linked to the COSMIC REALMS

> ORIGINAL ARTWORK TITLE: *UNIVERSAL HEALING SHIELD*

(THE HEALING SHIELD SERIES)

THE KEY ENERGIES:

The Universal Healing Shield is linked to the Cosmic Realms. At the core, the center of the soul, therein resides a most brilliant light composed of the purest and highest frequencies of love. This inspirational force is but a spark of the very matrix of Universes, cosmic matter, and is directly connected to the All-That-Is. Creatorship energy provides a constant and steady stream of cosmic connection that nourishes and feeds all souls with a fountain of radiance . . . and a pure refined stream of golden unity.

THE ORACLE INTERPRETATION:

Confronting the very core of yourself and your soul is the Universal Shield's greatest lesson. The main properties of this shield are the following:

- Initiates connection, alignment, and unity with the soul and Higher Self
- Infuses empowerment frequencies into all chakra fields
- Promotes feelings of courageousness, positivity, confidence, and safety

Your situation requires reconnecting with your Higher Self for answers. Do not look outside yourself, since you will be misled. Feeling fearful or indecisive? Flood your energy field with your own soul essence. Remember your power. Your situation is also asking for a healthy dose of positivity. See the beauty in all challenging situations and embrace these as opportunities, rather than hindrances. Choose the path of higher consciousness in all decisions. When you feel lost, bask in the sunlight of your own soul and return to your center.

REALIGNMENTS:

Meditation; Sungazing; Monoatomic Gold Ormus; Sweetgrass Smudging; Colors of Gold and White; Sunflowers; Frankincense and White Lotus Essential Oils; Elecampane and Golden Iris Flower Essences; Crystals of Golden Healer Quartz and Tiger's Eye

INNOCENCE
Unicorn Love

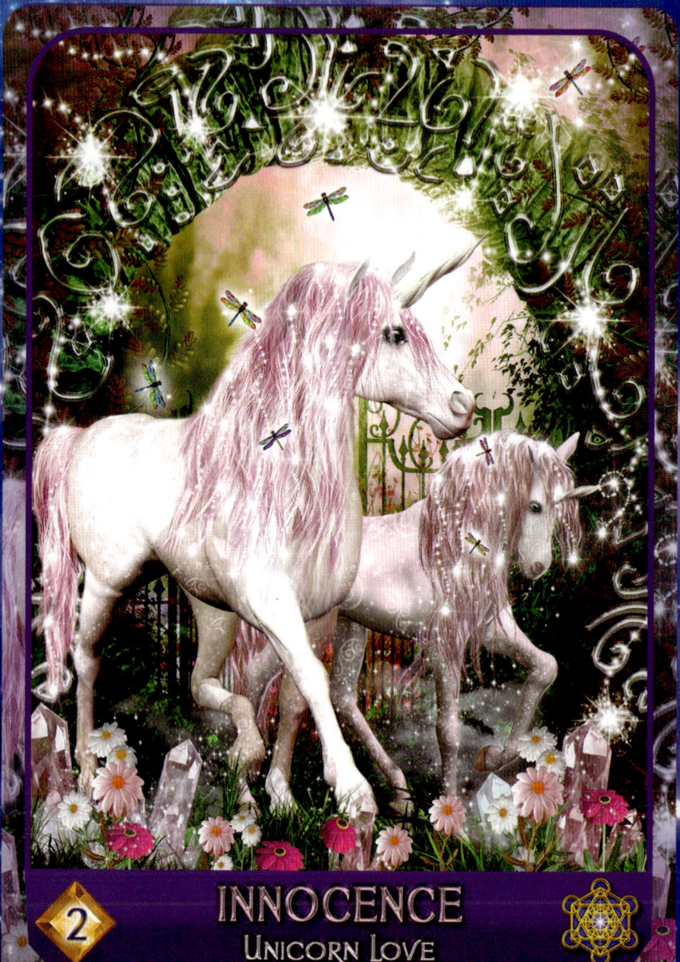

METATRON'S CUBE

2. INNOCENCE

ORIGINAL ARTWORK TITLE: *UNICORN LOVE*

THE KEY ENERGIES:

The beauty and enchantment of the Unicorns invites a charm into your life, for Unicorns draw all of their powers from faith, and they will inspire this within you. These mystical creatures hold only the highest frequencies of truth, love, and purity, and they embody the divine essence in the most pure and natural state. Shift your perspective and honor your own divinity and be a catalyst to allow magic, miracles, and healing to be realities in your life.

THE ORACLE INTERPRETATION:

Release all uncertainties by focusing on your own "magical horn" that will dissolve insecurities and doubts. Unicorns will open your imagination, allowing you to see into the worlds of mystery, and will also grant you great healing powers. The world of fairies, sprites, and magical things is waiting to open to you with beauty and wonder. Place more attention within your heart and the love that purely flows through you, and less attention on matters outside yourself. Assess your intentions and note if you have been participating and engaging in life from a place of divinity and virtuousness. Unicorn love, magic, healing, enchantment, and wisdom will be bestowed upon those who are pure of heart and virtuous in their deeds. Be childlike and BELIEVE once again!

REALIGNMENTS:

Heart Meditation; Magic and Mystical Studies; Visionary Films; Unconditional Love; Animal and Nature Therapies; Childlike Play; Faerie and Elemental Communication; Colors of Pink and Green, Pink Lotus and Vanilla Essential Oils; Orchid and Pink Daisy Flower Essences; Crystals of Rose Quartz and Green Aventurine

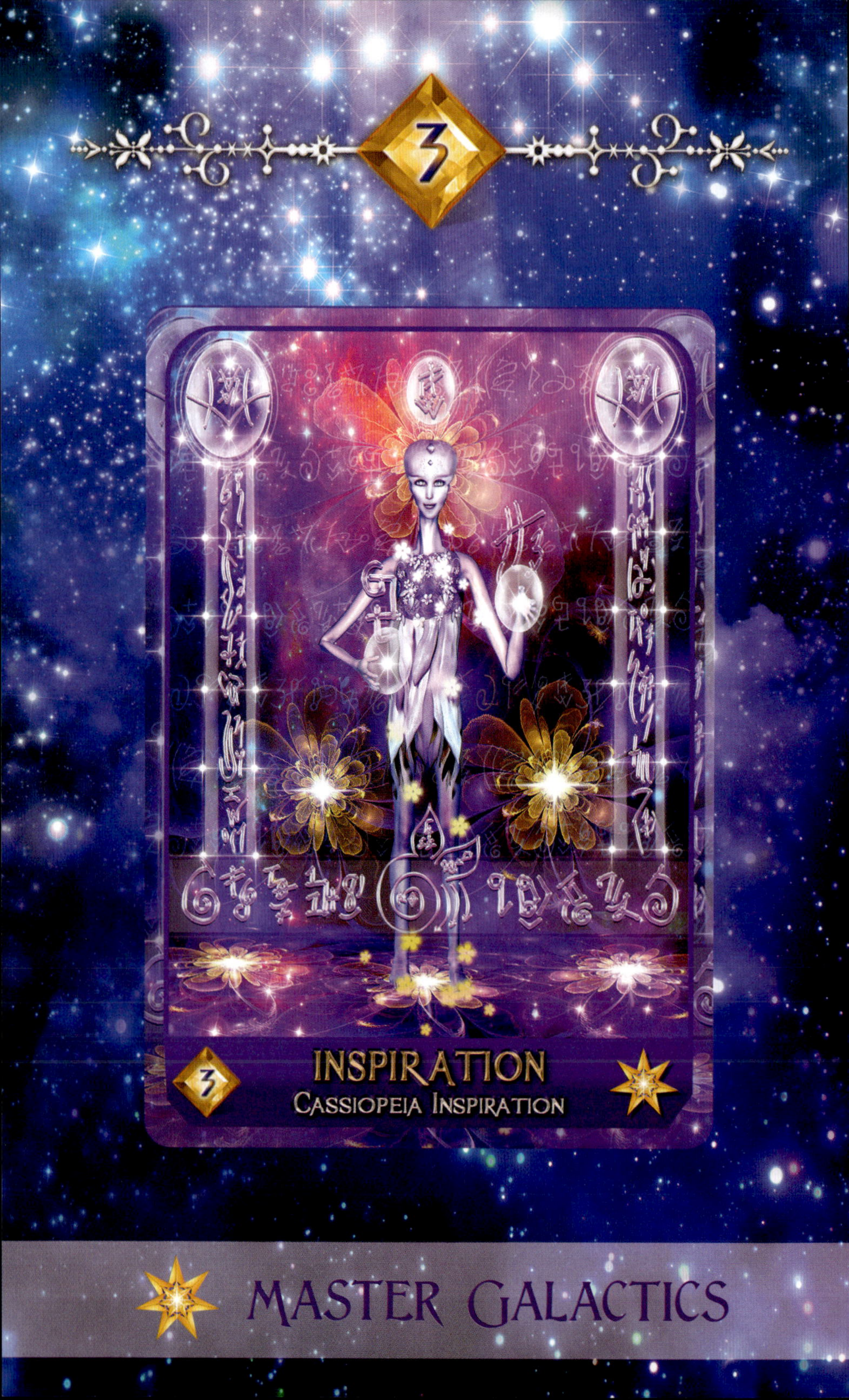
3
INSPIRATION
CASSIOPEIA INSPIRATION
3
MASTER GALACTICS

3. INSPIRATION

> ORIGINAL ARTWORK TITLE: *CASSIOPEIA INSPIRATION*

THE KEY ENERGIES:

With a warm embrace, the energies of Cassiopeia fill the air with love, life, and creative spirit. Expansive within all realms of the natural elements, most specifically flowers, we connect closely with magical life-giving energies, which emulate beauty and creation. Our nature is gentle and patient. We are immensely compassionate, and we initiate inspired ideas to encourage unique forms of expression. Our vast network of communities focuses on cultivation of progressive forms of art, science, music, and healing. When we share our spark of life, it can greatly lift your spirits, as we consciously serve as a beacon of inspiration . . . much like a creative muse.

THE ORACLE INTERPRETATION:

The loving qualities of Cassiopeia can help restore depleted energies back to a place of inspirational balance. If you have lost your zest for life or feel depressed, lethargic, or just apathetic . . . now is the time for a lift. Go outside into nature and be one with the flowers and trees. Sit under a tree and journal some inspired ideas from nature. If you are feeling unmotivated, a rejuvenating rest in the nature elements will revive you. At this time, you can benefit greatly from engaging an art or music therapy project . . . photography, pastels, acrylic, watercolor, graphics, toning, singing . . . the important thing is to allow the richness and depth of your spirit to be expressed through a creative outlet. You could use a positive sacred space to release your built-up stressful tension so you can regain a sense of well-being.

REALIGNMENTS:

Nature Walks; Journaling; Art Therapy; Music and Sound Healing; Colors of Fuchsia and Gold; Bergamot and Citrus Essential Oils; Buttercup, Fire Star Orchid, and Clematis Flower Essences; Crystals of Rhodochrosite and Ametrine

4

ACCELERATION
417 Hz Cleansing Healing Code

THE HEALING CODES

4. ACCELERATION

Shifts negative or self-sabotaging subconscious programming and inspires creativity

Associated with the SACRAL PORTAL (Chakra)

Original Artwork Title: *417 Hz Cleansing Healing Code*

(The Healing Code Series)

THE KEY ENERGIES:

The Healing Code Series includes potent healing codes that resonate to specific Solfeggio tones and contain visual-activation properties. Solfeggio frequencies make up the ancient six-tone scale thought to have been used in sacred music, including the beautiful and well-known Gregorian chants. The chants and their special tones were believed to impart spiritual blessings when sung in harmony. Each Solfeggio tone is composed of a frequency required to balance your energy and keep your body, mind, and spirit in perfect unison. Experiencing the vibration of these frequencies in the form of visual art enhances these tones, forming an alchemical healing activation for the soul.

THE ORACLE INTERPRETATION:

The Cleansing Healing Code resonates to the Solfeggio tone of 417 Hz, which balances the energy center of the sacral chakra. This energetic code fosters purification and change. It stimulates inner cleansing by initiating an energetic bath of balance, joy, and clarity of expression. It facilitates healing from trauma, stepping out of the shadows into the light. Ask yourself what feels toxic in your internal or external environment. Cleanse your home, body, or workspace from electromagnetic radiation, or toxic emotions in the air. You may need to take a breather before you can more effectively address your situation with grace and ease. Put your inner smudge stick to good use!

REALIGNMENTS:

Sacral Chakra; 417 Hz Solfeggio Tone; Detox Baths; Emotional Clearing; Sage or Palo Santo Smudging; Colors of Golden Yellow and Orange; Lichen and Black Locust Flower Essences; Lemon and Orange Essential Oil; Crystals of Smoky Quartz, Orange Carnelian, and Citrine

TRANSITIONS
Karmic Timeweaver

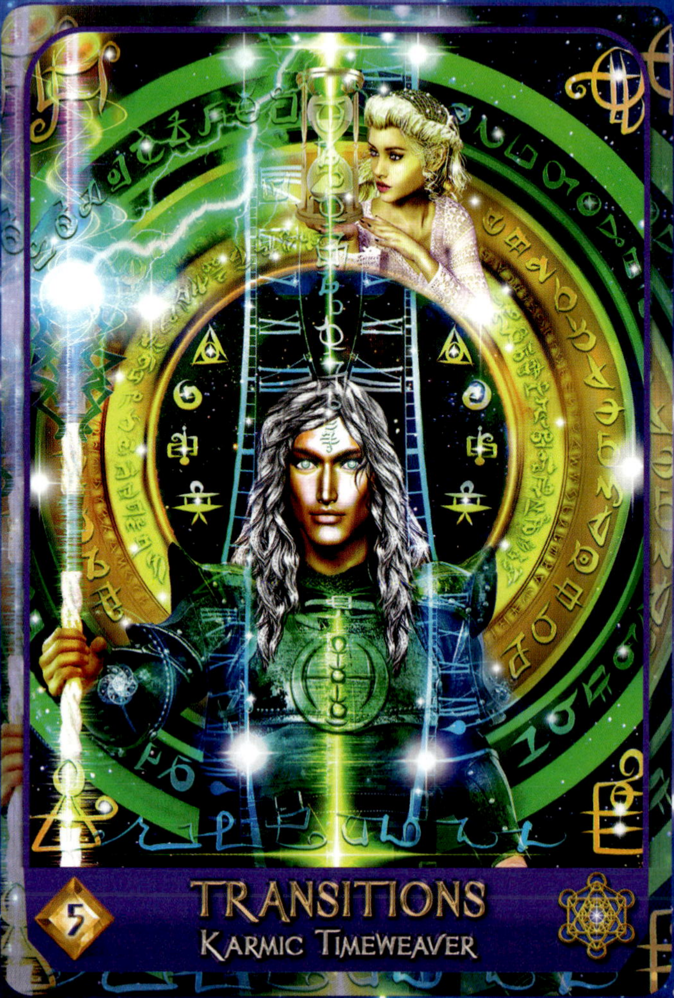

METATRON'S CUBE

5. TRANSITIONS

Original Artwork Title: *Karmic Timeweaver*

THE KEY ENERGIES:

Time is a paradox. Reality does exist in the "now moment"; however, events can appear to occur in a linear timeline. To grasp the concept of time is to experience consciousness in its most expanded state, as a perception of the unlimited soul, and an expression of space itself. Multiple timelines exist concurrently, which breathes life into concepts of individual choice, cause and effect. One may not be consciously aware of each and every decision made in all the various timelines, but when they intersect, as a mighty matrix, a web of consciousness is created . . . bridged together in an ever-united grid of quantum energetic exchange.

THE ORACLE INTERPRETATION:

The Karmic Timeweaver brings an abundance of change. Decisions will need to be made swiftly. This may involve a geographical move, relationship adjustments, health decisions, spiritual changes, or a career shift. Although there are no right or wrong outcomes, it will be imperative that you make choices in alignment with your soul, since your decisions may have karmic impacts for others in your past, present, and future timelines. So, evaluate carefully. The Timeweaver connects you with otherworldly realms, and karmic ties, which can bring fresh insights into your own Akashic records. Greet upcoming transitions with excitement; they will help you settle unresolved karmic entanglements. Significant opportunities may emerge that will forever alter your life. You may be faced with making an unexpected decision that may not seem to make logical sense. It is okay. Trust yourself to align with the best decision for the higher good of all.

REALIGNMENTS:

Past-Life Regression; Life-Transitions Coaching; Quantum Healing; Mullein Leaf Smudging; Patchouli Incense; Colors of Emerald Green and Gold; Holy Basil and Astragalus Herbs; Nutmeg and Spearmint Essential Oils; Aspen and Walnut Flower Essences; Crystals of Chrysocolla, Malachite, and Elestial Quartz

6

BOUNDARIES
Empath Healing Shield

THE HEALING SHIELDS

6. BOUNDARIES

To support and **reestablish** healthy, emotional boundaries, strengthen the bioenergetic field, and dissolve emotional toxicity
Linked to the EMOTIONAL REALMS

ORIGINAL ARTWORK TITLE: *EMPATH HEALING SHIELD*

(THE HEALING SHIELD SERIES)

THE KEY ENERGIES:

The Empath Healing Shield is linked to the Emotional Realms. One of the gifts embedded within the human form is the wide spectrum of emotions. But the most extraordinary gift is the ability to exemplify mastery in the midst of chaotic emotional terrain. The capacity to receive, feel, and flow within a storm of emotion, while refraining from absorbing the entire bandwidth, is true mastery. Reacting from a place of acceptance, detachment, balance, and compassion is what is required for high-frequency emotional processing.

THE ORACLE INTERPRETATION:

Healthful processing and expressing emotions are the Emotional Shield's greatest lessons. The main properties of this shield are the following:

- Prevents absorbing excessive emotional baggage from others
- Dissolves internal and external toxic and negative emotions
- Promotes healthful boundaries and open communication

Do you feel excessive emotional tension? Are you overwhelmed by other people's emotions? It is time to wring out your inner emotional sponge. Your true feelings about a situation may be hidden, so honesty with yourself is in order. You will benefit from assertively expressing your emotions in a healthful manner. If you suspect narcissists or energy vampires in your midst, quickly establish boundaries; don't allow them to feed on your energy. Empower yourself with clarity of your emotional terrain and react with mastery.

REALIGNMENTS:

Bioenergetics; Hydrotherapy; Chi Gong; Palo Santo Smudging; Colors of Lavender and Blue; Geranium and Chamomile Essential Oils; Pink Yarrow and Red Chestnut Flower Essences; Crystals of Hematite and Amethyst

7

PERCEPTIVITY
Psychic Healing Shield

THE HEALING SHIELDS

7. PERCEPTIVITY

To initiate and **reignite** intuitive abilities, heighten extra sensory perception, and shield from psychic attack
Linked to the MENTAL REALMS

ORIGINAL ARTWORK TITLE: *PSYCHIC HEALING SHIELD*

(THE HEALING SHIELD SERIES)

THE KEY ENERGIES:

The Psychic Healing Shield is linked to the Mental Realms. Thoughts are manifestations of the projected reality. So, the phrase "You create your own reality" is absolutely true. To create a healthful mental outlook is to be aware of outbound projected thoughts, and also inbound receptive thoughts. Fragmented human thought projections, the collective consciousness, or dark entities can become lodged in the mental field and can cause disruption and unclear, negative, and scattered thought forms. Being diligently aware of this is key to embodying a calm and positive mind.

THE ORACLE INTERPRETATION:

Proactive awareness and shifting your mental thought patterns is the Psychic Shield's greatest lesson. The main properties of this shield are the following:

- Invites positivity and infinite possibilities into your mental energy
- Promotes intuitive awareness, clarity, focus, and creative vision
- Blocks psychic attacks and lower vibrational negative thought forms

This is a good time to make optimism your mantra. Refuse to succumb to any thoughts that are depressive, destructive, or negative. Psychic attacks from lower-frequency beings may be trying to embed anger, fear, self-doubt, and confusion in your mind. Do not allow this to penetrate your inbound field. If you are feeling anxious or unclear about your situation, infuse a flow of positive vibrations to promote clear thinking. This is important, so do not delay.

REALIGNMENTS:

Mindful Meditation; Positive Affirmations; Breathwork; Eucalyptus Smudging; Colors of Violet and Silver; Mint and Lavender Essential Oils; Clary Sage and Lupine Flower Essences; Crystals of Azurite and Fluorite

8

SOVEREIGNTY
Orion Magical Creation

MASTER GALACTICS

8. SOVEREIGNTY

Original Artwork Title: *Orion Magical Creation*

THE KEY ENERGIES:

We are the Orions, the keepers of magical realms and light-based ancient wisdoms. We embrace a sacred connection to all planets within the cosmos, and we are master manifestors in the etheric and physical realms. Emanating confidence, courageousness, strength, and resiliency, our intentions are in alignment with the cocreative universal love of the Prime Creator. We are the Warriors of Truth, Wizards of Light, and Time Lords who originally seeded the realms of magic in many Universes. We serve not to overpower—but to empower. For eons of time in the past, dark forces have corrupted and misused our energies, but we continue to hold a torchlight of truth, infinitely empowered by love . . . forever and in all dimensions.

THE ORACLE INTERPRETATION:

The Orion energies will help strengthen your manifestation abilities. Have you forgotten who you are? You are a powerful force of light in this world—remember this. If you have been feeling helpless in your situations, it is time for a boost of empowerment. All the resources you need are inside you, but you must access them. Do not allow yourself to be overwhelmed or controlled by others in any way. Be assertive. You create and manifest your own reality and can change the circumstances, people, and places in your life, merely by shifting your perceptions. Be mindful of whom you attract into your energy field, and intuit their intentions. It may also be time for you to step forward into the unknown and journey into that long-overdue Knight's Quest.

REALIGNMENTS:

Wizardry Apprenticeship; Leadership Training; Manifestation Techniques; Colors of Gold and Emerald Green; Tibetan Bowls; Black Seed Oil, Oil of Oregano; Agrimony and Mimulus Flower Essences; Black Spruce and Elemi Essential Oils; Crystals of Black Tourmaline, Smoky Quartz, and Citrine

9

CONSCIOUSNESS
Ascension Healing Shield

The Healing Shields

9. CONSCIOUSNESS

To **restore** and deepen spiritual connections with the Angelic Realms, Spiritual Guides, and Ascended Masters
Linked to the SPIRITUAL REALMS

Original Artwork Title: Ascension Healing Shield

(The Healing Shield Series)

THE KEY ENERGIES:

The Ascension Healing Shield is linked to the Spiritual Realms. The purpose of the soul is to experience while expressing an expanded version of Divine love. Along the path of spiritual ascension, a variety of spiritual tests exist, in order for the soul to have ample opportunities for expansion. Some opportunities are preordained, while others occur spontaneously, but there is always assistance from the higher realms, and being able to discern high-frequency from low-frequency energies is critical.

THE ORACLE INTERPRETATION:

Discernment and experiencing higher-frequency energies are the Ascension Shield's greatest lessons. The main properties of this shield are the following:

- Enhances alignment to high-frequency Angels, Spiritual Guides, and Masters
- Infuses ascension path codes with Divine love, passion, and purpose
- Dissolves old contracts and misalignments blocking spiritual progression

Are you living, or merely just existing? If you feel like something is missing in your life, now is the time to turn in a more spiritual direction. The answers you seek require understanding from a much-higher perspective than what you currently perceive. Your Angelic and Spiritual Guides are ready and waiting to assist you. Remember discernment and invite guidance only from the highest echelons of love. If you have been lacking passion or purpose, the solution resides in expansion of your spiritual focus and trying something new.

REALIGNMENTS:

Ascension Meditation; Angel Oracle Cards; Chakra Balancing; Mugwort Smudging; Colors of Hot Pink and Gold; Angelica and Rose Essential Oils; Orchid and Red Rose Flower Essences; Crystals of Kunzite and Auralite

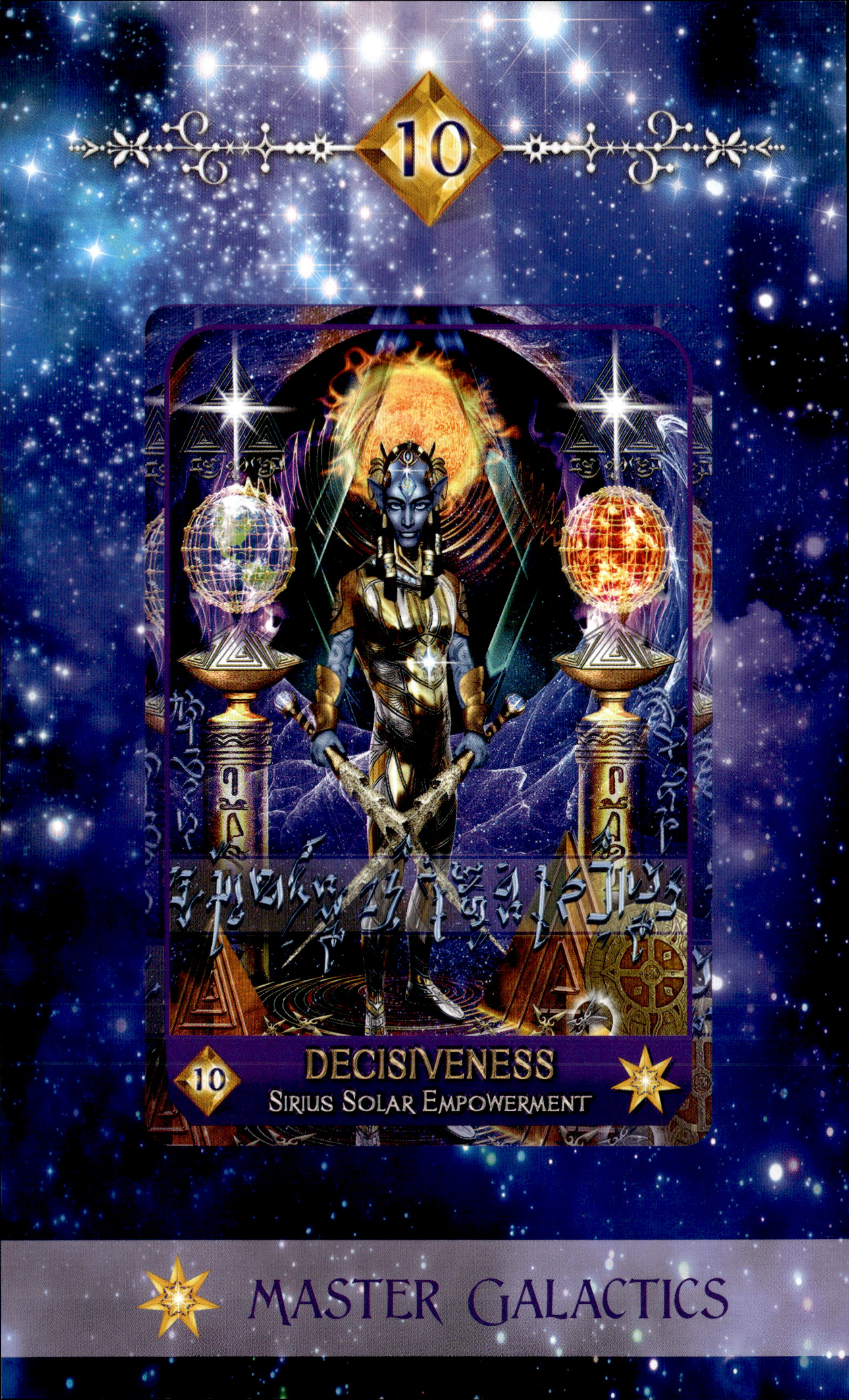
10
10
DECISIVENESS
SIRIUS SOLAR EMPOWERMENT
MASTER GALACTICS

10. Decisiveness

Original Artwork Title: *Sirius Solar Empowerment*

The Key Energies:

We are the Sirian Warriors of Light. We serve many worlds in times of planetary transformation and ascension. By stimulating gridular leylines, we help realign and anchor in new pillars of light that awaken and activate empowerment codes within all living beings. As planets prepare to transition into new levels of ascension, our Sirian codes assist with balancing the planetary meridians and infuse them with potent solar energy frequencies. By nature, we are powerful healers, and guardians of ancient spiritual technologies that upgrade, activate, and realign the crystalline grids, DNA, and holographic templates.

The Oracle Interpretation:

You are ready to work with the action energies of the Sirian frequency codes, which will help you become more assertive with resolving your current situation. If your health is challenged, get ready to receive a potent dose of healing energy. If you are feeling insecure or have suppressed your light, simply open the throat chakra and speak your truth. Emotions may feel more intense than usual, but this is to be expected, since it initiates self-awareness. You are experiencing a profound inner transition, and it's time for action. Time to "terraform" your life by removing the old paradigm and building the new. You may benefit greatly right now from activating and recharging your energy from Gaia, and the solar rays of the sun.

Realignments:

Throat Chakra Clearing; Sungazing; Holographic DNA Upgrades; Planetary Leyline Clearing; Egyptian Gematria; Colors of Blue, Indigo, and Orange; Chrysanthemum and Wild Oat Flower Essences; Cinnamon and Peppermint Essential Oils; Crystals of Lapiz and Orange Carnelian

11. LOVE

> **Original Artwork Title:** *Pleiades Star Angel*

THE KEY ENERGIES:

Galactic Blessings from the Star Angels of the Pleiades, where the magic of your heart and emotional healing become one. Voyage to our higher-dimensional-frequency healing system of light to transform emotions. We generate an upsurge of healing that enters your emotional heart to help with expansion and transmutation of negativity. We harness the magical power of the seven-pointed star that becomes the bridge of spiritual evolution for all sentient beings.

THE ORACLE INTERPRETATION:

Receive the energetic shower and loving star-fire power of the Galactic Pleiades Angels, as they pour a vessel of love into your heart to elevate and restore balance. It's time to address your emotions and receive assistance from these highly evolved Master Star Healers. Allow the Star Matrix and the Divine Light Codes from the Angels of the Pleiades to form a channel between the light of The Creator and your heart. They will help you feel comforted and nurtured in times of emotional stress, and particularly when you feel stuck in lower vibrations. Welcome new creative ideas and inspirations to come flooding into your auric field to uplift your spirits and wash away feelings of sadness, grief, and loneliness. You are a child of light and need a reminder that all is well. You are infinitely loved and supported.

REALIGNMENTS:

HeartMath Techniques; Forgiveness Rituals; Deep Breathwork; Pleiadian Angel Connection; Seven-Pointed Star; Colors of White, Purple, and Blue; Jasmine and Acacia Flower Essences; Rose and Violet Essential Oils; Crystals of Rose Quartz, Blue Fluorite, and Amethyst

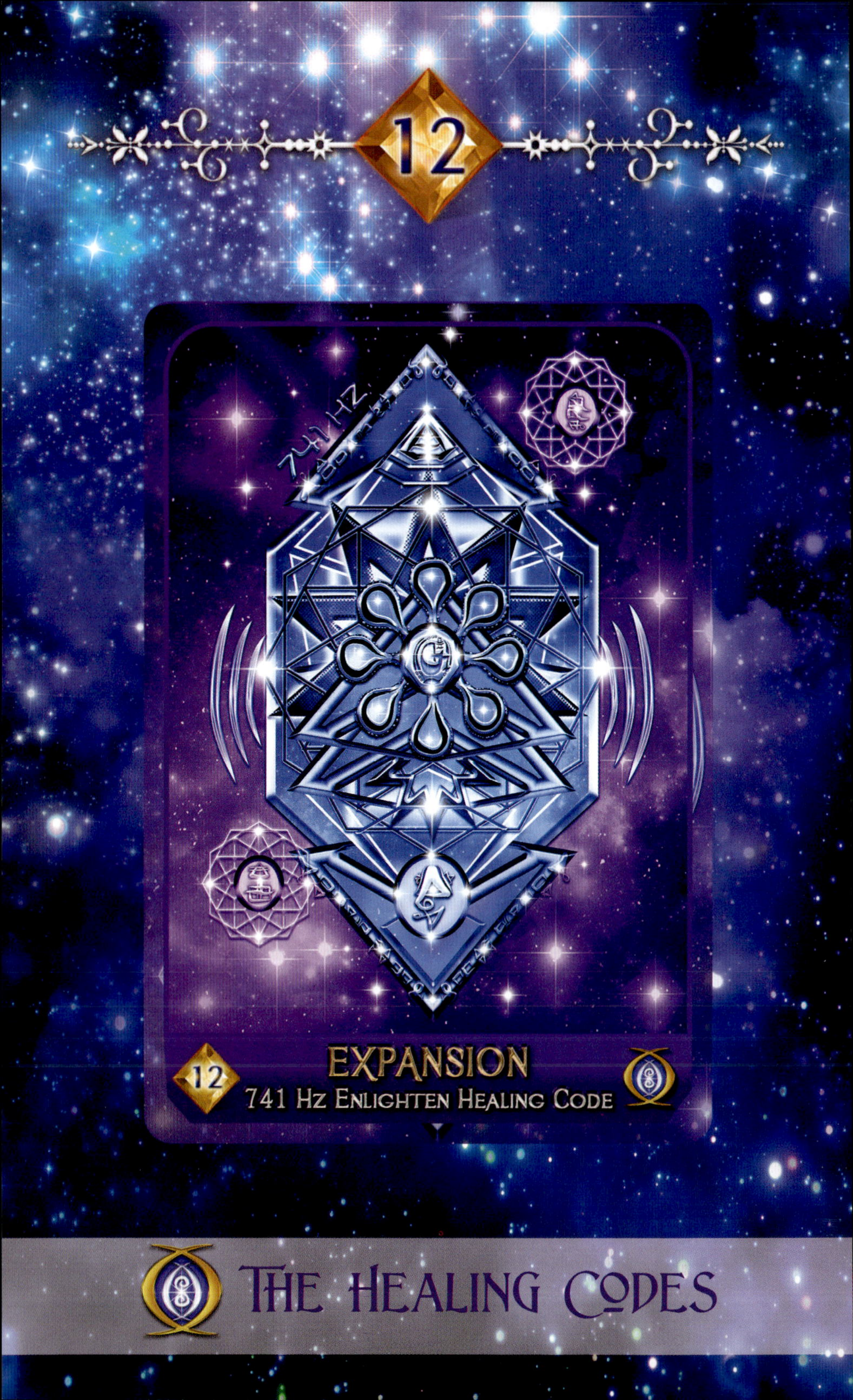

12

EXPANSION
741 Hz Enlighten Healing Code

THE HEALING CODES

12. EXPANSION

Supports purification, clear communication, and assertiveness
Associated with the THROAT PORTAL (Chakra)

Original Artwork Title: *741 Hz Enlighten Healing Code*

(The Healing Code Series)

THE KEY ENERGIES:

The Healing Code Series includes potent healing codes that resonate to specific Solfeggio tones and contain visual-activation properties. Solfeggio frequencies make up the ancient six-tone scale thought to have been used in sacred music, including the beautiful and well-known Gregorian chants. The chants and their special tones were believed to impart spiritual blessings when sung in harmony. Each Solfeggio tone is composed of a frequency required to balance your energy and keep your body, mind, and spirit in perfect unison. Experiencing the vibration of these frequencies in the form of visual art enhances these tones, forming an alchemical healing activation for the soul.

THE ORACLE INTERPRETATION:

The Enlighten Healing Code resonates to the Solfeggio tone of 741 Hz, which balances the energy center of the throat chakra. This precious code expands communication and raises spiritual awareness to divine truth. Your situation will benefit greatly from being open to new pathways of connecting with others. Step beyond your comfort zone, because you are ready to speak your truth, and perhaps with a more healthful, creative, diplomatic, and higher vibe. It may feel uncomfortable, but you know the truth, which will provide all the grace you need. Trust in the answers you receive; you got this!

REALIGNMENTS:

Third-Eye Chakra; 741 Hz Solfeggio Tone; Automatic Writing; Crystal Therapies; Channeling; Public Speaking; Colors of Light Blue and Lilac; Star Tulip, Violet, and Himalayan Blue Poppy Flower Essences; Blue Lotus and Lilac Essential Oil; Crystals of Kyanite, Amethyst, and Herkimer Diamond

13. DISCERNMENT

Original Artwork Title: *Vega Fearless Journey*

THE KEY ENERGIES:

We are the Spiritual Bridge, Navigators, and WayShowers of the many dimensional realms. Step into potent self-awareness with the assistance of the Galactic Guides from Vega. We help realign those who are scattered, splintered, or trapped in fear. We are Masters of discernment, second sight, and are symbiotically connected with the Natural World and the Animal Kingdoms. Call on us to confront fears, phobias, the shadow self, the subconscious, or negative energies. Access the supraconsciousness and return to your natural state of crystal-clear inner guidance.

THE ORACLE INTERPRETATION:

Let's dive deeply into the root of your situation. Is there something you've been avoiding? Have you been feeling lost, frazzled, scattered, or confused? Need a course correction back to your power? Never fear, the WayShowers of Vega are here. It's time to put the pieces of the puzzle together. But first, you'll need some courage. Being assertive can sometimes feel uncomfortable, but you are being asked to face your fears and know the truth of your situation. This is not a time to sit on the sidelines. Action is required, and you are being prompted to open your eyes to gain hidden insights beneath the surface. Be diligently aware and discerning about who (or what) is in your energy field right now. This is a good time to release situations that feel heavy. Discover and call on power animals to assist; they have important messages for you. Pay close attention to your dreams.

REALIGNMENTS:

Shamanic Journeying; Dream Journaling; Animal Totems; Sage and Cedar Smudging; Colors of Midnight Blue and Turquoise; Blue Tansy and Sage Essential Oil; Rock Rose and Aspen Flower Essences; Crystals of Boji Stone and Merlinite

14

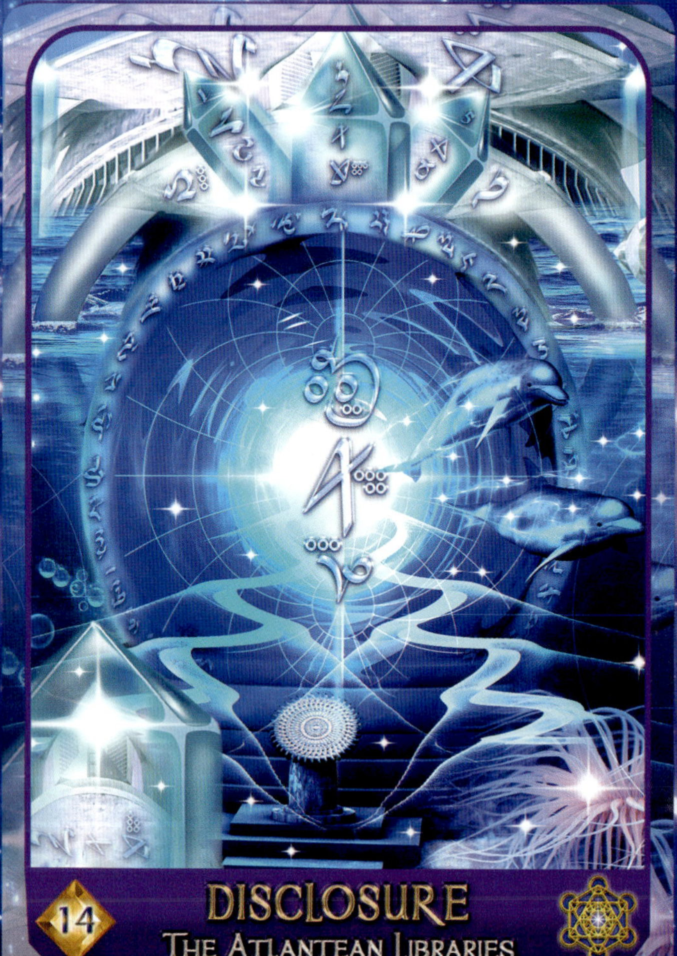

DISCLOSURE
The Atlantean Libraries

METATRON'S CUBE

14. Disclosure

Original Artwork Title: *The Atlantean Libraries* (Panoramic)

THE KEY ENERGIES:

Welcome to the Aqua-Gate . . . the passageway within the mystical waters of the Jewel of Terra, to a network of neural libraries. It is known in the terrain of aquatic cities as the Atlantean Libraries, a specialized connective tunnel system of shared knowledge and intelligence, which provides certain dispensations to the bearers of particular DNA codes. To reach the libraries, one must first receive clearance through an encoded gateway before entering the Main Hall of Records. Multiple access points are then linked to the ancient archives and the holographic intelligence. This is a sacred place for discovery, knowledge, wisdom, and sharing.

THE ORACLE INTERPRETATION:

Do you hear an inner calling for spiritual knowledge? It is time to embark upon an important quest for truth, wisdom, and connectivity with other like-minded souls. You may be feeling a yearning to gather more closely with the intergalactic star teams, your soul star family, or your earthly soul family. You may be pulled toward exploring sacred truths about the mysteries of the Earth, the Universe, and beyond. Get ready for more. If you are sitting on the sidelines, rise and step forward. Engage. Your answer is yes—travel down that rabbit hole, deeper toward the truth; you are going in the right direction. However, if you feel stagnation, or as if you've spiritually plateaued—be adventurous, try a new path, and take a leap into the vast unknown. Although you may not know the final destination, your bravery to explore is worth taking that journey. You are ready to receive, learn, and upgrade.

REALIGNMENTS:

Guided Visualizations for Courage; Shamanic Journeys; Scuba Diving; Traveling; Dolphin Therapy; Salt Crystal Baths; Colors of Midnight Blue and Mint Green; Blue Yarrow and Wintergreen Essential Oil; Larch and Mountain Forget-Me-Not Flower Essences; Crystals of Blue Lace Agate and Green Beryl

15

COMPASSION
639 Hz Love Healing Code

THE HEALING CODES

15. COMPASSION

Inspires gravitation toward high frequencies of love, compassion, and harmony
Associated with the HEART PORTAL (Chakra)

Original Artwork Title: *639 Hz Love Healing Code*

(THE HEALING CODE SERIES)

THE KEY ENERGIES:
The Healing Code Series includes potent healing codes that resonate to specific Solfeggio tones and contain visual-activation properties. Solfeggio frequencies make up the ancient six-tone scale thought to have been used in sacred music, including the beautiful and well-known Gregorian chants. The chants and their special tones were believed to impart spiritual blessings when sung in harmony. Each Solfeggio tone is composed of a frequency required to balance your energy and keep your body, mind, and spirit in perfect unison. Experiencing the vibration of these frequencies in the form of visual art enhances these tones, forming an alchemical healing activation for the soul.

THE ORACLE INTERPRETATION:
The Love Healing Code resonates to the Solfeggio tone of 639 Hz, which balances the energy center of the heart chakra. This code uniquely initiates and enhances emanations of love and high heart frequencies and fosters healthful relationships. Allow balance, connection, harmony, and positivity to take center stage in your life. Be inspired to open your heart toward giving, receiving, and positive communication. Dissolve blocked or suppressed emotional pain and be replenished with a frequency tone that paves a Divine pathway back to the higher frequency that you are. Choose to recall the power of love into your reality in the moment, regardless of circumstance.

REALIGNMENTS:
Heart Chakra; 639 Hz Solfeggio Tone; Emotional Expression; Charity/Humanitarian Work; Deep Breathwork; Colors of Green, Pink, and Fuchsia; Rose and Lily Flowers; Neroli Essential Oil; Helichrysum Essential Oil; Crystals of Green Aventurine, Emerald, and Malachite

16. WONDERMENT

Original Artwork Title: *Orb Healing*

THE KEY ENERGIES:
We are known as the Healing Orbs, geometric spheres of light that emanate healing energy and vibrational codes. Working as "Angelic energy cleansers," our light-filled geometric patterning is encoded with specific keys within the matrix of our core. These concentric keys contain codices of universes, planets, and a variety of species' DNA. Our key codes can analyze the status of wellness within any living being, and we can then bifurcate into microspheres, thus becoming "field scouts" that locate areas of imbalance and help restore homeostasis. We are here to help, and we serve with love.

THE ORACLE INTERPRETATION:
The world is filled with many wonders that cannot be easily explained by our third-dimensional existence. Many realities we encounter surpass the norm and defy logic. The multidimensional spectrum of the Healing Orbs awaits your self-discovery and awakened state of consciousness. So open your eyes; both eyes, that is. You may not be seeing your situation clearly and may be missing the fundamentals, that which is right in front of you. Could it be that you are already amid a rainfall of answers? Yes, so it may be time for a vibrational recharge after the rainfall. See your life as a dimensional snapshot of the divine and know that healing and answers are already present. Healing may come from the most unusual places, so never underestimate your abilities to see that which exists beyond the veil. Be open to receive the unexplainable.

REALIGNMENTS:
Angel Communication; Detoxification Therapies; Bubble Baths; Colors of Violet, Blue, and White; Hydrangea and Dandelion Flowers; Lilac and Lavender Essential Oils; Ball-Head Waterleaf and Angelica Flower Essences; Crystals of Clear and Purple Quartz Spheres, and Cat's-Eye Celestite Sphere

17

REJUVENATION
Purification Healing Shield

The Healing Shields

17. REJUVENATION

To help with **rebalancing** the third dimension, clearing toxins, cellular nourishment, and reclaiming abundance and prosperity codes
Linked to the PHYSICAL REALMS

Original Artwork Title: Purification Healing Shield

(The Healing Shield Series)

THE KEY ENERGIES:

The Purification Healing Shield is linked to the Physical Realms. If you peer through the physical world through a glass lens, it is perceived either as abundant or deficient, depending on who is looking through the lens. Perceptions of abundance expedite healing, while adopting an outlook of deficiency will decrease abundance. Thus, cultivating a viewpoint of infinite bounty when connecting with the physical body, healing, or manifesting abundance on the Earth plane is crucial. The optimal choice is clear.

THE ORACLE INTERPRETATION:

Nourishing your biology and your relationship to abundance is the Purification Shield's greatest lesson. The main properties of this shield are the following:

- Supports optimal cellular cleansing and releasing of toxins and waste
- Fortifies the physical body with vitality, regeneration, and loving support
- Fosters an overall perception toward abundance and prosperity

Have you been running on empty? You may be feeling depleted at the biological level. It will benefit you to take time to rest, cleanse, regenerate, and revitalize your body. Look within and reprioritize what might be neglected . . . YOU. Where is the nourishment in your life? You may also need to shift your perspective toward acknowledging the abundance and opulence in ALL life, so you can heal whatever feels inadequate, lacking, or depleted in your situation. Provide love and nourishment for your body and watch your life begin to flourish.

REALIGNMENTS:

Earthing Systems; Gardening; Yoga; Herbology; Lemongrass Smudging; Colors of Green and Orange; Tangerine and Neroli Essential Oils; Vervain and Oak Flower Essences; Crystals of Green Aventurine and Orange Carnelian

18

INITIATION
Valion The Wisdom Keeper

METATRON'S CUBE

18. INITIATION

> ORIGINAL ARTWORK TITLE: *Valion The Wisdom Keeper*

THE KEY ENERGIES:

From the very wisps of time and beyond these sacred lands, there exists a magnitude of knowledge . . . an ancient wisdom that is under careful watch. I am Valion, returning from a time of the first Ancient Dragon Orders of the Wisdom Keepers. My DragonKind shares the task of serving as a bridge that weaves ancient wisdom together with other species of enlightened evolution. Through crystalline skull structures and action blueprints, we link the Time Lords of Old with the Wizards of New. For those who are ready to begin their journey to accept, wield, safeguard, and transfer this power of knowledge, we now activate and release your ancient wisdom codes.

THE ORACLE INTERPRETATION:

You have the opportunity to embark upon a great mission. A dispensation awaits you—one that will awaken dormant light codes within. You hear the whispers of "the Call" within your soul for something greater. If you are lost, it is time to ground into your deepest levels of truth. There is a great force and strength behind you, prompting quiet reflection. Be still and know, and carefully assess your present situation. Be conscious and discerning of your intentions before taking action. Be focused and diligent and extract the nuggets of truth in your situation. You are entering a time of deep spiritual integration, so be receptive to synchronicities that may lead you on a deep and meaningful inner quest to relinquish old patterns of procrastination. The time for downloading and awakening your ancient wisdom has now begun!

REALIGNMENTS:

Crystal Skull Activation; Traveling to Sacred Sites; Ancient Practices; Shamanic Journeying; Colors of Silver, Blue, and White; Silver Fir and Camphor Essential Oils; Silversword and Cerato Flower Essences; Crystals of Septarian or Galena

19

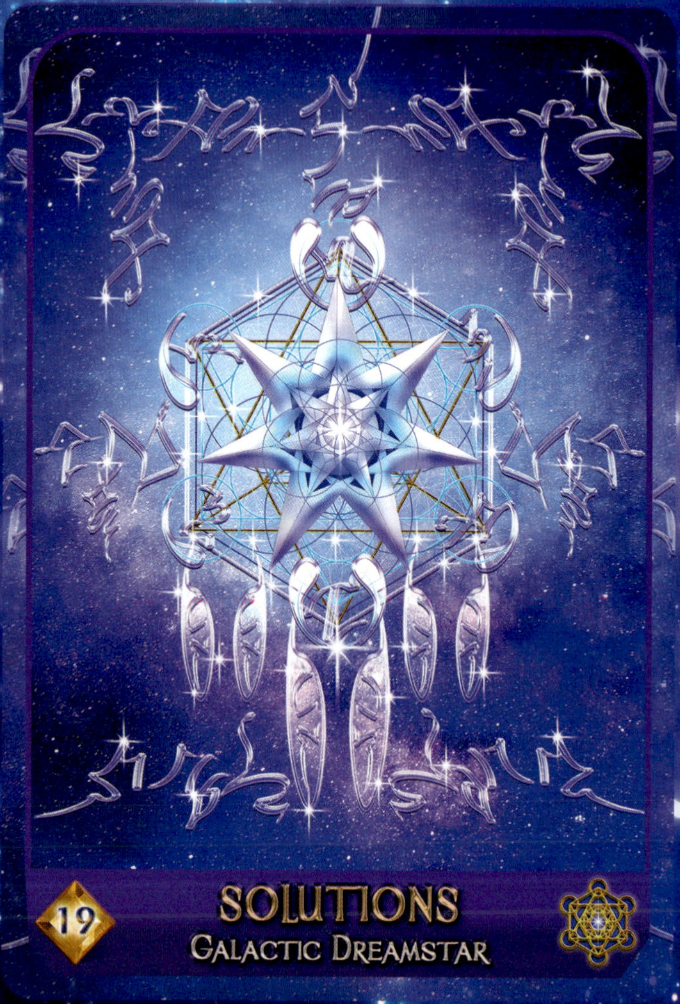

SOLUTIONS
Galactic Dreamstar

METATRON'S CUBE

19. SOLUTIONS

ORIGINAL ARTWORK TITLE: *GALACTIC DREAMSTAR*

THE KEY ENERGIES:

Does the Dreamer walk in reality, or in the illusion? There is a grand voyage that exists in the realm of dreams. This is a special place where the mysteries of the soul's path can be experienced most fully. It is within the exciting journey of the malleable matrix of the very fabric of time that you become truly empowered. From weaving the most-intricate dreamworld tapestries, solving challenges, becoming empowered, and healing at the core, a "Sacred Dreamometry Map" is created, one that inspires connectivity to one another, and ultimately to the All-That-Is.

THE ORACLE INTERPRETATION:

Your soul is expanded in your dreamtime and becomes replenished in this enhanced state, where you can experience your natural form more fully. Pay attention to your dreams more carefully at this time. You may receive an answer in your dreams, as if a lightbulb turned on. So, give yourself a break from overextending your mental field, trying either to solve a problem or overworrying about a situation. Relax, let go, and open up to the possibilities of spontaneous dream solutions. You may need some extra integration time for day or night dreaming or rejuvenation sleep (or both). Listen, and allow for this. Dream enhancement codes will help you decipher and be empowered by the content of your dreams, and to break free of confusion. Engage in lucid dreaming and never forget your innate power to alter your reality.

REALIGNMENTS:

Shamanism; Dream Journaling; Lucid Dreaming; Mugwort Smudging; Colors of Ultra Violet, White, and Lavender; Thyme, Lavender, and Valerian Essential Oils; Passionflower and Alpine Aster Flower Essences; Crystals of Herkimer Diamond, Amethyst, and Shamanic Dreamstone

20

RESILIENCE
Lyra Genesis Activation

MASTER GALACTICS

20. RESILIENCE

Original Artwork Title: *Lyra Genesis Activation*

THE KEY ENERGIES:

We are the Lyran souls, the ones who hold the very matrix and seeds of the planetary predecessors of your world. Our lineage spans time far beyond your known realms and is diverse and unique in its patterning. Carrying the human genetic codons, we anchor DNA codes of powerful light within your core. We have traversed many trials and tribulations, since our many worlds have been destroyed, and yet we continue to emerge, resurrect, and flourish with the strength of the Ancients. Our connections run deep, since we are infused with the very life force of creation, with nature realms anchored within our essence. We breathe life and passion as our natural soul expression.

THE ORACLE INTERPRETATION:

The brilliant codes from the Lyrans will deeply reconnect you to your own Ancestors, and the true origins of your soul. Whenever you feel tired and want to give up the fight for life, remember—you are stronger than you realize. Reach into the very core of your soul, the warrior spirit, and know that you have everything you need within you to emerge from difficult and challenging situations. You are eternal and have access to the very creative life force within you to persevere and never give up. Your situation requires tenacity and the drive to emerge from the darkness, to teach and lead from experience, and to be inspired from the story of your own life. You are being called to balance and harmonize your Divine Feminine and Masculine within. Your DNA is being activated; strengthen the power within you now.

REALIGNMENTS:

Warrior Training; DNA Activation; Earthing; Firewalking; Colors of Orange and Earthy Tones; Orange and Tangerine Essential Oils; Oak and Carnation Flower Essences; Crystals of Orange Carnelian, Amber, and Mookaite Jasper

21

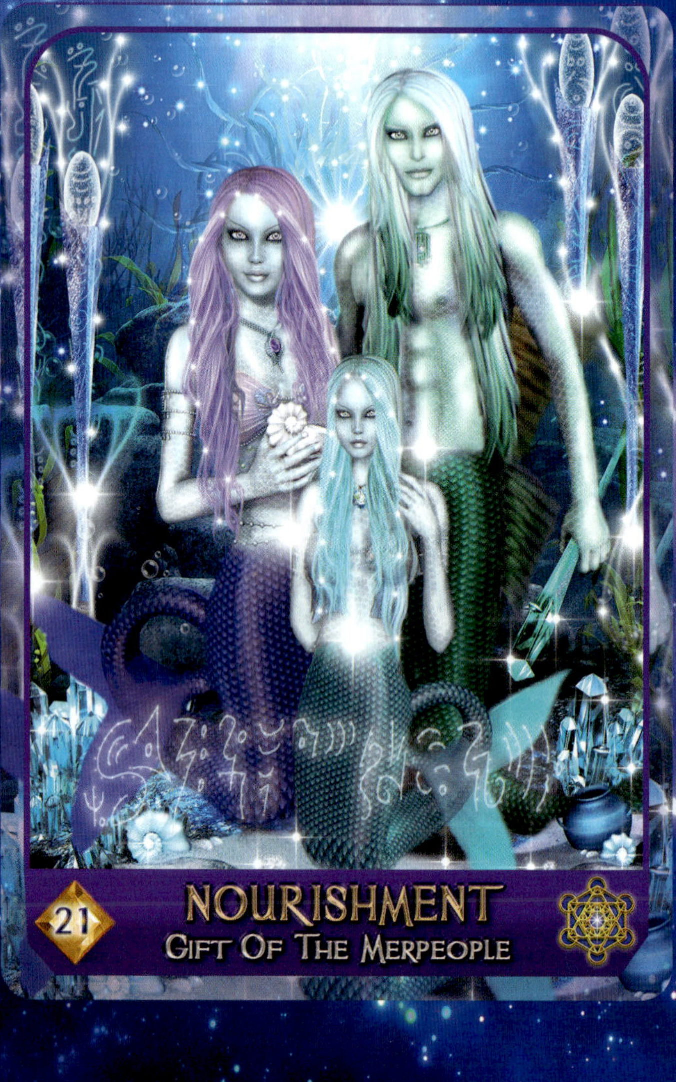
21
NOURISHMENT
GIFT OF THE MERPEOPLE

METATRON'S CUBE

21. NOURISHMENT

ORIGINAL ARTWORK TITLE: *GIFT OF THE MERPEOPLE*

THE KEY ENERGIES:

Open your heart to receive the precious gift from the Merpeople of the sea. These beautiful souls are aligned with water elements and assist with purification of the body, and releasing and cleansing of toxic emotions. Dive into the terrain of your life to discover blocked emotions and explore the depths of these waters more deeply. Allow these emotions to bubble to the surface for detoxification and transmutation. "Let your hair down" and breathe into life once again. Release aggravated energies that feel tense and restricted, and bring awareness to situations where you are being rigid or stubborn. It's now time to go with the flow, rather than fighting against the tides.

THE ORACLE INTERPRETATION:

The healing properties of the ocean are very therapeutic, but if you cannot be at the sea, immerse yourself into a relaxing sea salt bath; it will make a world of difference. And while you bask in this tranquil state, visualize these alluring Mer creatures of the sea bathing you with nourishing love and healing light. Plunging deeper into your subconscious memories, you may recall a connection to the Merpeople from the seas of the Sirius Constellation, Atlantis and Lemuria, or on other planets and universes. Be open to their supportive, healing, playful, and loving energies.

REALIGNMENTS:

Sea Salt Baths; Trace Minerals and Kelp; Aquatic Exercise; Hydrotherapy; Detoxification; Tears; Ocean Vacations; Colors of Aqua Blue and Teal; Blue Chamomile and Juniper Essential Oils; Crab Apple and Australian Bottle Brush Flower Essences; Crystals of Aquamarine, Larimar and Fuchsite

22

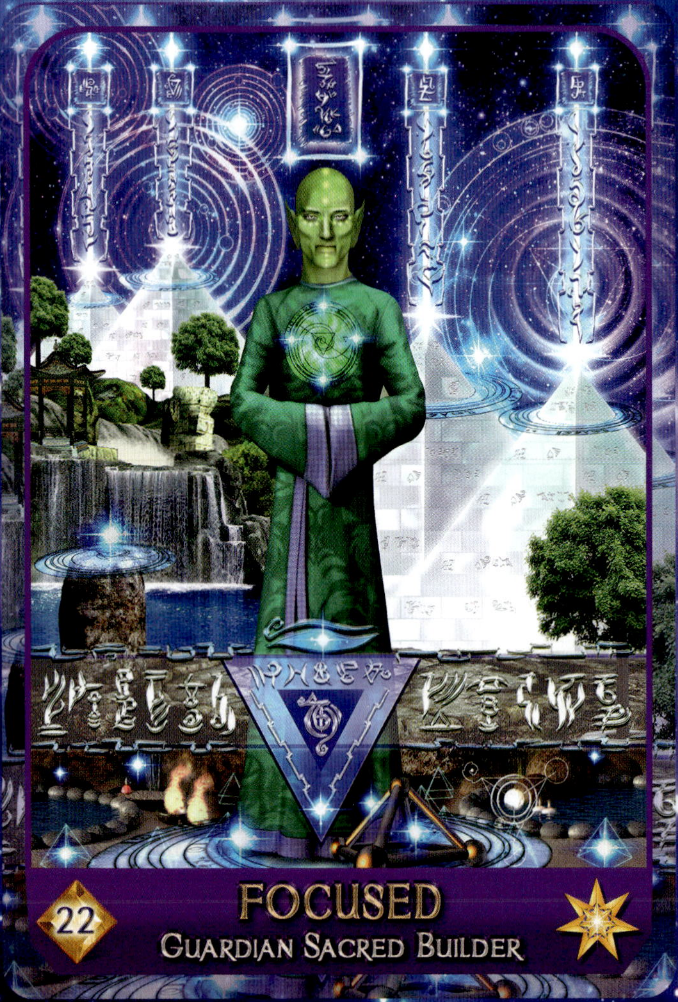
FOCUSED
22
GUARDIAN SACRED BUILDER

MASTER GALACTICS

22. Focused

Original Artwork Title: *Guardian Sacred Builder*

THE KEY ENERGIES:

We are known as The Guardians, a conglomeration of various races charged with specific missions relating to the guardianship and harmonization of planetary bodies and star systems. Serving as an intergalactic coalition, we are the diplomatic negotiators, blueprinters, and balancers, who are often referred to as the "Master Builders" or "Ancient Builder Races." We specialize in planetary templating using mathematical blueprinting, quantum science, vibrational healing, and sacred geometries of light to create planetary structural balance. However, we also provide arbitration to restore equity and fairness in times of galactic unrest.

THE ORACLE INTERPRETATION:

You are receiving divine quantum light codes that will help with rebalancing instability, and thus this timeline of contemplation will require strategic planning, designing, and refinement. Linking with The Guardian's harmonizing energies infuses sacred codes to initiate expansion of inspirational new projects, transformational career shifts, communication enhancement, or shifting health concerns. First, assess and take inventory. Does your situation require new development, restoration, or rebuilding? Or do you need an entire overhaul? Be honest. Hidden messages are about to be revealed, so pay attention. Concentrate and focus on the highest good for all involved. Then, draft and INvision your alchemical blueprint to activate your high-frequency creation template.

REALIGNMENTS:

Sacred Geometry; Vision Boards; Quantum Resonance; Automatic Light Code Script Writing; Sandalwood Incense; Colors of Light Blue, White, and Violet; Rosemary and Buddha Wood Essential Oils; White Chestnut and Cosmos Flower Essences; Crystals of Blue Quartz and Purple Fluorite

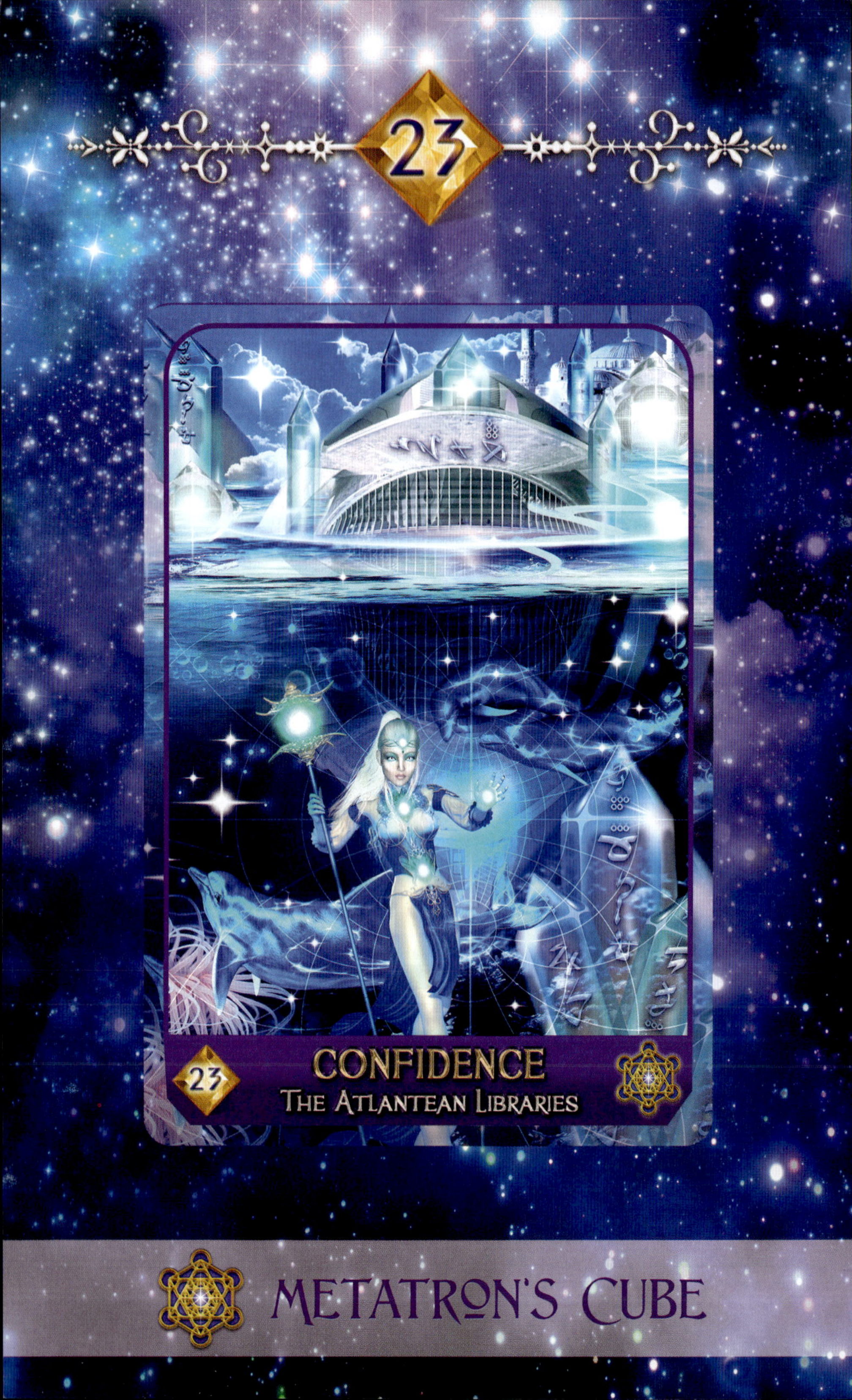
23
CONFIDENCE
THE ATLANTEAN LIBRARIES
METATRON'S CUBE

23. CONFIDENCE

ORIGINAL ARTWORK TITLE: *THE ATLANTEAN LIBRARIES*
(PANORAMIC)

THE KEY ENERGIES:

When you feel lost, distracted, or off path, these are all a part of your internal barometer, your soul signaling to you that something is off balance. Traverse beneath the surface and dig deeper, deeply past all the mind chatter. You will hear a gentle whisper beckoning you back to yourself. This whisper may arise from within the soul, or from a trusted navigator in spirit, to gently empower and nudge you to trust your internal navigation system. Have confidence and align with your inner truth in knowing which pathway to take. Trust your internal guidance.

THE ORACLE INTERPRETATION:

You already have the answers. Listen, trust your intuition, and have faith in yourself. Doubtfulness serves no purpose; honor the guidance you are receiving. Your spiritual guides are assisting with whispers of truth, to direct you back in alignment. Do not ignore or shun the subtle signs and messages you receive. They are valid. Check your energy stream and reestablish a strong connection, because your internal guidance is trying to relay some important messages. Are you paying attention, or have you been distracted? If you feel unplugged, identify what has interrupted the connection to your higher alignment. There is always a beacon to show you the way home. Seek the light within. Second-guessing yourself, insecurities, and feelings of unworthiness only serve to delay answers. You are a spark of the love and light of The Creator, and confidence naturally flows within you.

REALIGNMENTS:

Spirit Guide Communication; Intuitive ESP Training; Crystal Chakra Alignments; Developing Trust; Dolphin Healing; Colors of Silvery White and Royal Blue; Myrtle and Birch Essential Oils; Nigella and Hornbeam Flower Essences; Crystals of Amazonite and Sodalite

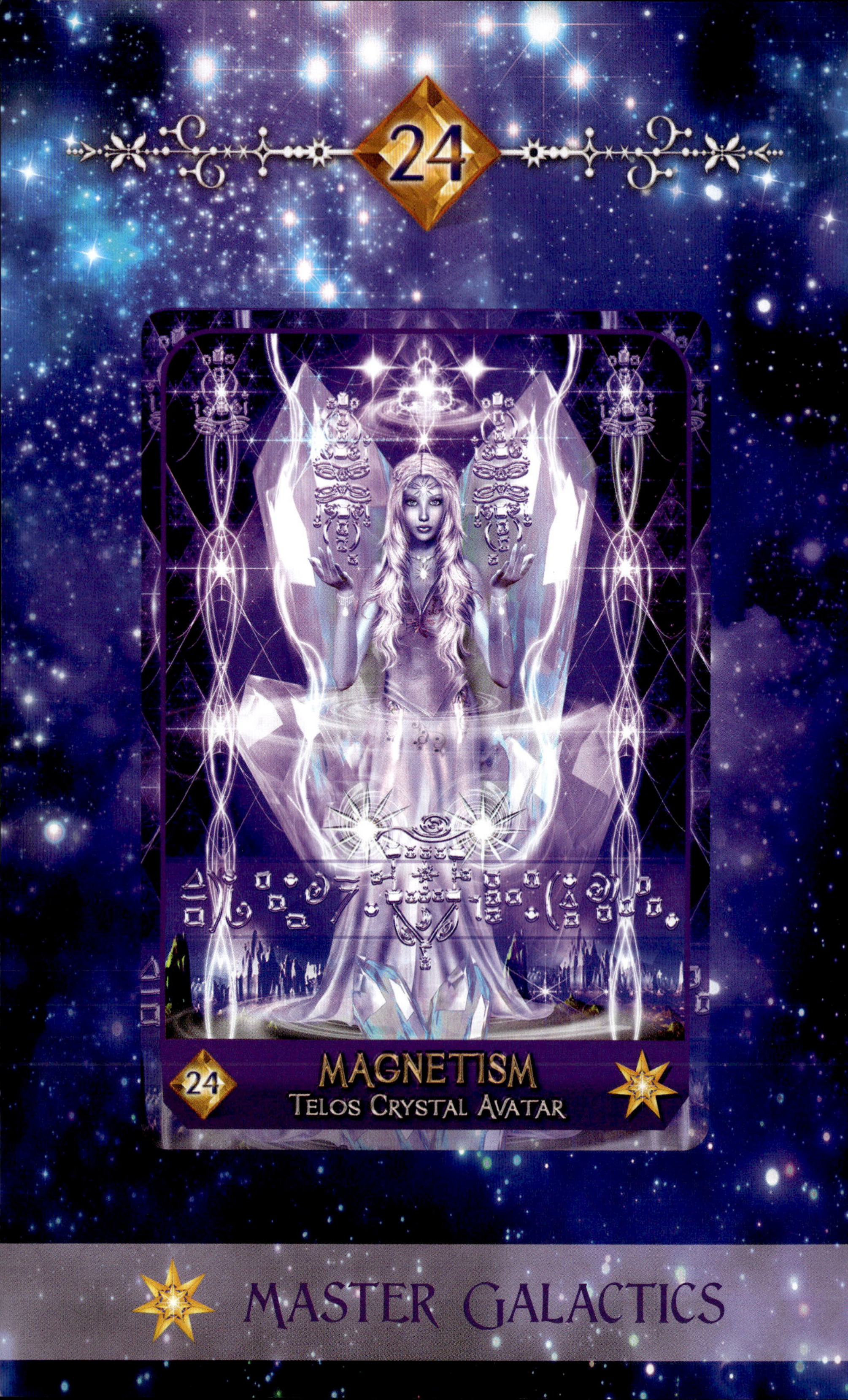

24
MAGNETISM
Telos Crystal Avatar

MASTER GALACTICS

24. MAGNETISM

Original Artwork Title: *Telos Crystal Avatar*

THE KEY ENERGIES:
Sending a blessed embrace from the crystal temples of Telos, we are the Crystal Avatars. Our energetic divine power creates a dynamic matrix of crystalline light, and we serve the cosmos by infusing our light into the auric fields of those open to receive. The source of our energies are contained within crystalline-based structures that reflect beauty, clarity, and strength. We embody the perfected state of refined frequencies, and working with us will assist you in clearing your spiritual channels and imbue a cleaner and refined energetic field.

THE ORACLE INTERPRETATION:
You are being guided to work with the Crystal Avatars from Telos and their crystalline realms for healing. You may be experiencing remnants of past negative programs that are circulating in your mental fields, which are subconsciously affecting your situation, emotions, or physical body. By working with crystal elements and currents, your auric field receives new upgrades and templates that magnetize, elevate, and enhance your energy. This will strengthen your overall outlook on your situation so you can make more-clear decisions. It's time to charge and resequence higher frequencies and new intentions directly into your crystals. Be open to receiving new vibrations via your subtle energy bodies, as you are growing more sensitive to vibrations around you. Purify your auric field clear from disruptive or destructive energies that may be hijacking or siphoning your energy.

REALIGNMENTS:
Salt Lamps; Drinking Water with Crystals; Crystal Bowls; Colloidal Silver; Colors of Violet and Lavender; White Angelica and Lilac Essential Oils; Violet and Pansy Flower Essence; All Crystals—Particularly Angel Aura

25

INNOVATIVE
ANDROMEDA HEALING MATRIX

MASTER GALACTICS

25. INNOVATIVE

Original Artwork Title: *Andromeda Healing Matrix*

THE KEY ENERGIES:

We, The Andromedans, expand and express our blessings of heart-filled love and peace. The Healing Matrix is not a place, or a thing, but rather an expression of the Divine unification within the very core of the living soul, spirit, and matrix of living form. Our energies emanate that of integrative healing, an essence that embodies harmony, peace, and high-frequency healing. We are a consciousness of Divine GeoHarmonics, and our sacred tones serve to heal and dissolve disharmony and chaos, while transforming density into light.

THE ORACLE INTERPRETATION:

The healing embrace of Andromeda greets you with a high-frequency dose of love, to remind your consciousness that YOU are the healing you seek. Transformation and regeneration exist within mere thought and initiation, so if you engage in focusing your positive intentions inward, you will discover your own healing matrix... which will clear confusion and doubt. Whether your situation is of a spiritual, mental, emotional, or physical nature, it matters not. If you tune into the song—the tones of your own soul—and the power within you, you can transform anything. There is no limitation. Believe in yourself and your abilities to shift the energy surrounding you and all who enter your healing matrix. You have healing abilities that await your discovery, and you are now ready for this awakening to commence. What you are about to embark upon requires courage, yes, indeed... but the rewards will be profound and fulfilling and will enlighten you to new heights of confidence, inner power, and peace.

REALIGNMENTS:

Music; Voice Toning; Sound Therapy; Sacred Geometry; Colors of Turquoise, Silver, and Blue; Blue Tansy and Blue Cypress Essential Oils; Stonecrop and Chicory Flower Essences; Crystals of Turquoise, Shattuckite, and Malachite

26 · PARTICIPATION
Elven Alchemy

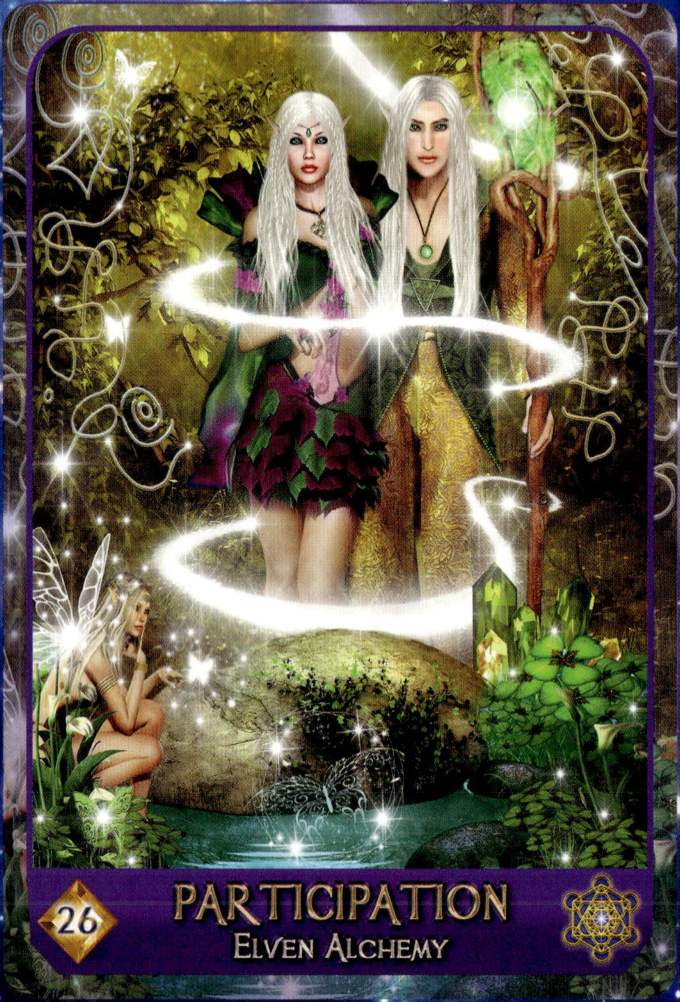

METATRON'S CUBE

26. Participation

Original Artwork Title: *Elven Alchemy*

THE KEY ENERGIES:

The enchanting realms of the Elven Kingdom are filled with ancient wisdom and powerful healing energies. Tied deeply with wondrous Inner Earth, and intertwined as the Agarthan beings, they are the great custodians of Mother Earth, endowed with transformative healing abilities. They are Great Earth Shamans trained extensively in the realms of herbs, flowers, crystals, the Devic worlds, and all of Mother Earth's natural medicines, which they utilize to create very high-frequency vibrational energy fields for healing purposes.

THE ORACLE INTERPRETATION:

Tune into the wisdom and expertise of the Elven Kingdom for assistance with crafting the healing you seek. These captivating beings await communication with you so they can share their gifts. They can teach you the ways of the Earthen Alchemist in order to heal your body, mind, and spirit. You are being guided by the Elven people, and their robust and potent forces will soon be transforming your situation into a new and higher frequency. Be ready to receive more vitality and Gaian wisdom. You are also being encouraged to spend more time in nature tuning in to the realms of Gaia for guidance. Listen. Practice using your intuition, allowing your internal compass to lead you, and make sure to follow through with any insights you receive.

REALIGNMENTS:

Gardening; Nature Walks; Tree Energies; All Botanicals and Herbs; Waterfalls; Code-Enhanced Purified Water; Leafy Green Foods; Patchouli and Vetiver Essential Oils; Shamrock and Sunflower Flower Essences; Crystals of Peridot and Serpentine

27

CURIOSITY
Zeta Spiritual Expansion

MASTER GALACTICS

27. CURIOSITY

Original Artwork Title: *Zeta Spiritual Expansion*

THE KEY ENERGIES:

We bring greetings of peace and love. We are known as the "Curious Ones" from Zeta Reticuli. With a varied and multilayered focus, we are teachers of advanced extrasensory perception, and we carry accelerated genetic blueprints for alchemical healing. Our skills and capabilities also include nervous-system repair and genetic hybridization. We frequently exchange technologies with other galactic races. Due to our inherent and controlled emotional nature, we strive for excellence and spiritual expansion.

THE ORACLE INTERPRETATION:

If you have been feeling confused, unclear, or insecure about your intuitive capabilities, now is the time to ignite your inner navigator with newfound Zeta-like enhancement. Exercise your extrasensory perception skills. Look at your situation from a more expanded perspective. Change your vantage point, and test your inner abilities. Open up to receiving spiritual data from alternative sources, especially those that stretch you out of your comfort zone. Be curious, and reach beyond what you think of as possible. However, be very aware of your energy! If you've been pushing yourself too far, give your mind and body a rest, especially to regenerate those frazzled nerves. You are transforming! Focusing on spiritual acceleration will activate your dormant DNA and help you gain new healing insights. Spiritual and alchemical upgrades await, so be sure to pave a pathway for assimilation of higher energies.

REALIGNMENTS:

Third-Eye Meditation; Light Therapy; Telepathic Exercises; Ascension Studies; Colors of Pink and Gold; Geranium and Pink Carnation Essential Oils; Pink Monkeyflower and Mimosa Flower Essences; Crystals of Kunzite and Spirit Quartz

28

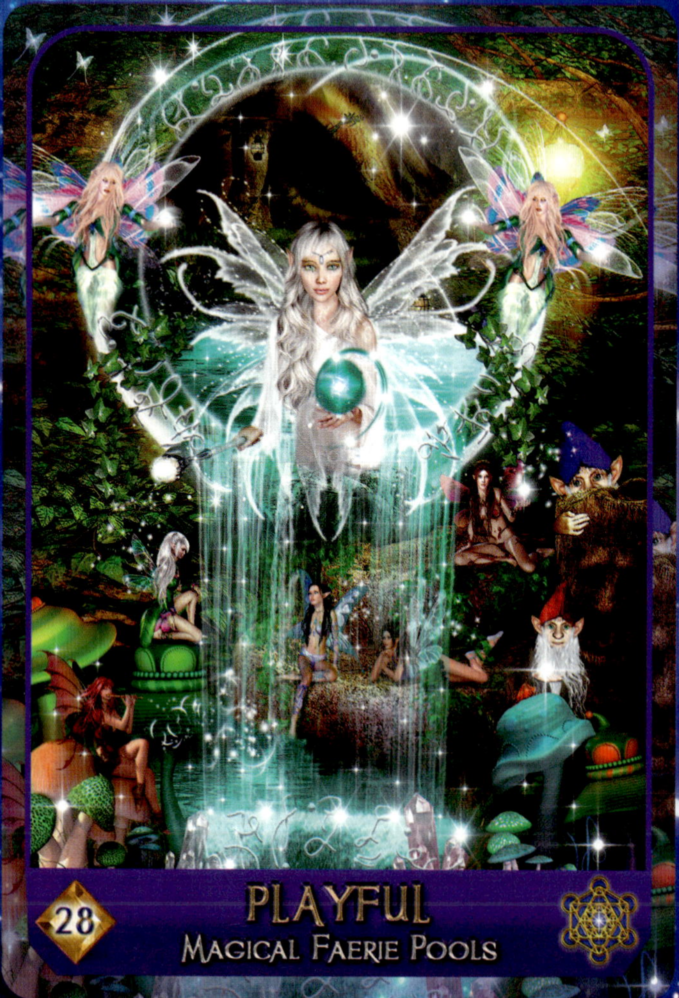

PLAYFUL
Magical Faerie Pools

METATRON'S CUBE

28. PLAYFUL

Original Artwork Title: Magical Faerie Pools

THE KEY ENERGIES:

The enchanting realms of the Faeries, filled with life, vibrancy, and aliveness. These magical and very precious beings of light are deeply connected to Mother Earth, since they are the custodians of the animals, plants, and elements on Earth. They lovingly tend and care for all living matter. These precious souls carry great powers amid their brilliant form. Their own magical creation, the ever-so-revered Faerie Dust, is composed of light particles and holds special powers that can heal, create, transform, and inspire.

THE ORACLE INTERPRETATION:

You could use a magical dose of Faerie Dust right now to lift your spirits and inspire you with lightheartedness and laughter. Sometimes the density of our 3-D life can make us feel weighed down with responsibilities or burdens, and we need to remember to breathe and have some fun. So, time to play in nature, swim in the creek, commune with the trees and flowers, and play with the Fairies and Gnomes. Take your mind off your woes and put your attention on becoming like a child at heart. Fly and be free. The Faeries carry such love and expressiveness in their hearts, and they are just waiting to light up your pathway with sparkles. Will you put your troubles aside just for a time and open your heart to a visit with the Faeries in their magical healing pools?

REALIGNMENTS:

Pine Forests; Running Streams; Music; Inner-Child Playfulness; Mushrooms; Chocolate; Colors of Sparkling Green and Gold; Cinnamon and Helichrysum Essential Oils; Pansy and Bluebell Flower Essences; Crystals of Faerie Quartz and Staurolite

REBALANCE
Astral Healing Shield

THE HEALING SHIELDS

29. REBALANCE

To **reorganize** and harmonize scattered or fragmented energies in the astral, auric, and etheric realms
Linked to the DIMENSIONAL REALMS

> ORIGINAL ARTWORK TITLE: ASTRAL HEALING SHIELD

(THE HEALING SHIELD SERIES)

THE KEY ENERGIES:

The Astral Healing Shield is linked to the Dimensional Realms. In the Astral Plane, both light and dark activities occur, so traversing dimensions requires auric strength and stamina, much like a rock that remains steady and grounded while rushing waters consistently roll across its back. In both the dreamtime and waking states, the auric field is being activated, so strengthening it will shield and deflect lower-dimensional fragments from attaching to your astral body and auric field.

THE ORACLE INTERPRETATION:

Building a healthy auric field and astral body is the Astral Shield's greatest lesson. The main properties of this shield are the following:

- Fortifies the etheric and astral bodies during dreamtime and waking states
- Promotes bonding to the lifeline cord, preventing premature detachment
- Deflects attachments from low-frequency dimensional entities

Vulnerabilities in your etheric or astral bodies may cause energetic weakness, like a slowly leaking balloon. Infuse your etheric body with a shimmering bath of ultraviolet light to strengthen your field. Your dreamtime is also vying for your attention, so focus on decoding and extracting solutions from your dreams. Become aware of your surroundings very acutely. Negative forces may be attempting to invade your energy field and weaken you, so fortify your aura and do not invite unwanted guests. This is not a time for denial or escapism. Your situation requires assertive and action-oriented empowerment.

REALIGNMENTS:

Himalayan Sea Salt Baths; Astral and Psychic Training; Binaural Beats and Isochronic Tones; Sage Smudging; Colors of Ultraviolet Purple and Silvery Blue; Sandalwood and Rosemary Essential Oils; Honeysuckle and Cantu Flower Essences; Crystals of Selenite, Spirit Quartz, and Ametrine

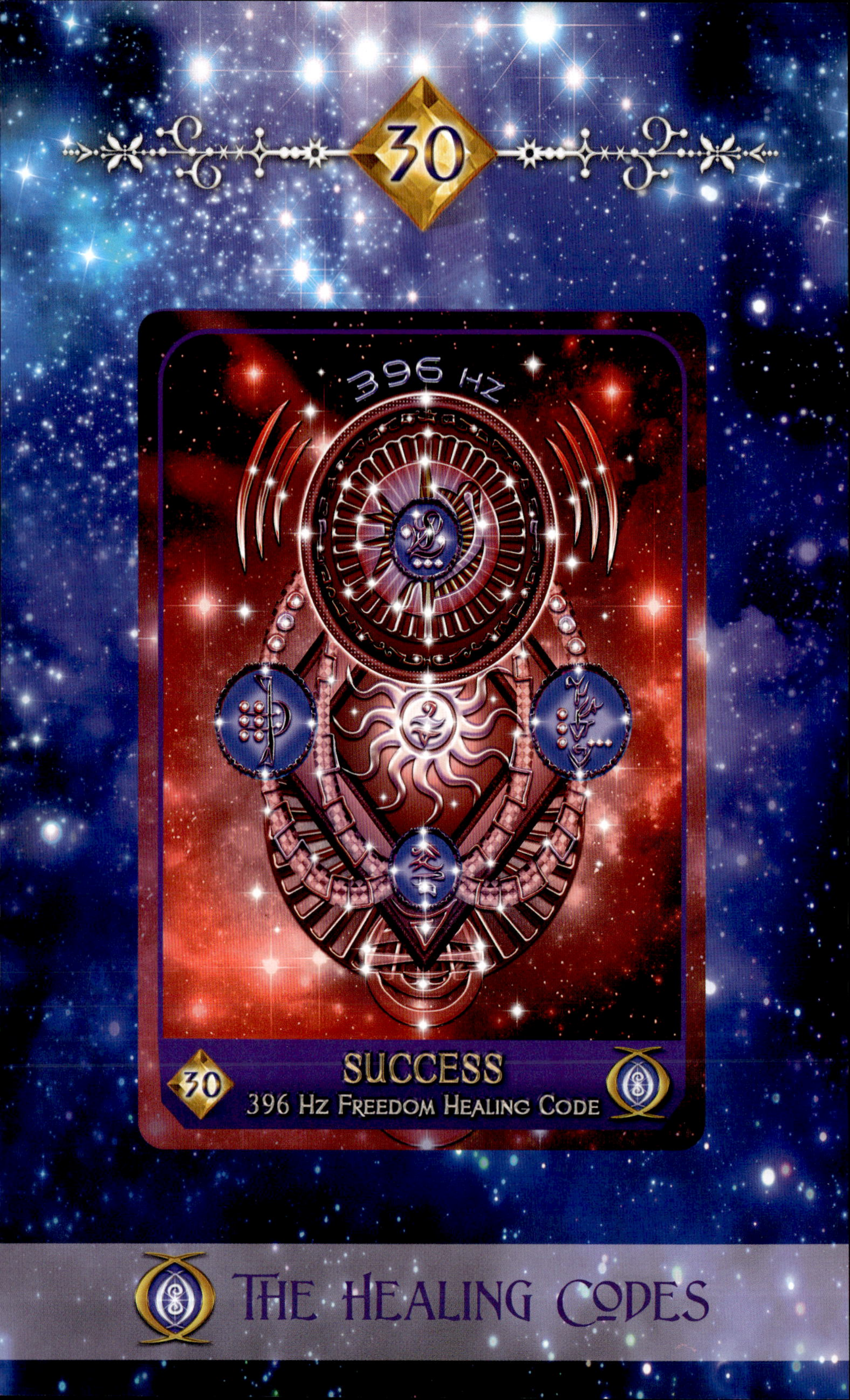
30
396 Hz
30
SUCCESS
396 Hz Freedom Healing Code
The Healing Codes

30. SUCCESS

Stimulates courage, groundedness, and the sense of triumph over obstacles
Associated with the ROOT PORTAL (Chakra)

Original Artwork Title: *396 Hz Freedom Healing Code*

(The Healing Code Series)

THE KEY ENERGIES:

The Healing Code Series includes potent healing codes that resonate to specific Solfeggio tones and contain visual-activation properties. Solfeggio frequencies make up the ancient six-tone scale thought to have been used in sacred music, including the beautiful and well-known Gregorian chants. The chants and their special tones were believed to impart spiritual blessings when sung in harmony. Each Solfeggio tone is composed of a frequency required to balance your energy and keep your body, mind, and spirit in perfect unison. Experiencing the vibration of these frequencies in the form of visual art enhances these tones, forming an alchemical healing activation for the soul.

THE ORACLE INTERPRETATION:

The Freedom Healing Code resonates to the Solfeggio tone of 396 Hz, which balances the energy center of the root chakra. This Healing Code provides a sense of empowerment and helps to be triumphant over obstacles. It is particularly helpful for transmuting feelings of guilt and fear, and raises your frequency to a higher octave of the notion of "I can" rather than "I cannot." Thus, this initiates a sense of liberation from negative beliefs and thoughts that can become deeply rooted or lodged within the subconscious. You are ready to assert yourself in a new and improved way. Your situation invites active participation in emitting a beacon of positivity.

REALIGNMENTS:

Root Chakra; 396 Hz Solfeggio Tone; Yoga; Brisk Exercise; Assertiveness Training; Deep-Tissue Massage; Colors of Red and Violet; Stargazer Lily and Pine Flower Essences; Cinnamon and Hyssop Essential Oil; Crystals of Ruby, Jaspers, and Sugilite

31

UPGRADES
LIGHTBODY SPECTRA

METATRON'S CUBE

31. UPGRADES

Original Artwork Title: *Lightbody Spectra*

THE KEY ENERGIES:

Your soul is initiating an integration process of the Spectra System of your Lightbody. As you shift into a higher-dimensional frequency of light, you are receiving a new brain in the nucleus of each cell in your body. Your cells are receiving a new intelligence, your DNA is upgrading, and as each cell advances and integrates the new tendrils of light, your body will have a heightened capacity to self-heal. These brilliant Divine Light Codes carry upgraded levels of healing, intuition, psychic energies, and extrasensory perceptions, including a new inner dialogue to monitor and direct specific quotients of energetic ascension within your own Lightbody.

THE ORACLE INTERPRETATION:

Your chakras are merging with one another, and this blending process is causing many shifts and changes. You are being realigned with a light matrix, so take extra tender loving care of your body. Get an abundance of rest, hydrate with healing fluids and nourishment, and allow both subtle and acute energetic shifts to be experienced. Love yourself completely through this process and have patience with your progression. Focus on grounding and breathing exercises to help you feel more peaceful and calm. Resistance to the integration process will only bring more challenges.

REALIGNMENTS:

Body-Focused Meditation; Rest and Relaxation; Yoga and Stretching; Trace Minerals; Colors of Ultraviolet Pink and Rainbow Colors; White and Pink Lotus and Gardenia Essential Oils; Tulip and Hibiscus Flower Essences; Crystals of Herkimer Diamond and Rainbow Fluorite

32

RECALIBRATION
Guardian Healing Shield

THE HEALING SHIELDS

32. Recalibration

To **reignite** and activate multidimensional communication with galactic family, starseed alliances, and celestial purpose
Linked to the GALACTIC REALMS

> Original Artwork Title: Guardian Healing Shield

(The Healing Shield Series)

THE KEY ENERGIES:

The Guardian Healing Shield is linked to the Galactic Realms. Interdimensional traveling within the galactic realms requires clarity and acute awareness. Subtle energies of portals and gateways can be opened that encourage extraterrestrial contact. These doorways can initiate downloads and transmissions, providing enhancement codes and upgrades that prepare biological life forms for spiritual progression. However, galactic missions also require recognizing safe ETs from those with negative ulterior motives.

THE ORACLE INTERPRETATION:

Initiating positive conscious interaction with otherworldly realms is the Guardian Shield's greatest lesson. The main properties of this shield are the following:

- Expands communication with love-based ETs and star family
- Invites The Guardians to initiate a supportive shield during connections
- Blocks negatively based implants and deflects lower-vibrational ETs

You are ready to connect with galactic aspects of yourself, so get prepared for extraterrestrial communication. However, proceed with caution in your approach . . . for you may encounter some unconventional concepts and some ETs with negatively based agendas along the journey. Have clarity and purpose with your quest before you embark upon it, and keep your shields up. If it is guidance you seek, you may receive otherworldly answers that have alternative perspectives, so be open to the information you receive.

REALIGNMENTS:

Stargazing; Astrology; Channeling; UFO Tours; Juniper Smudging; Colors of Gold, Silver and Red; Silver Fir and Black Pepper Essential Oils; Cosmos and Yucca Flower Essences; Crystals of Moldavite, Kyanite, and Pink Calcite

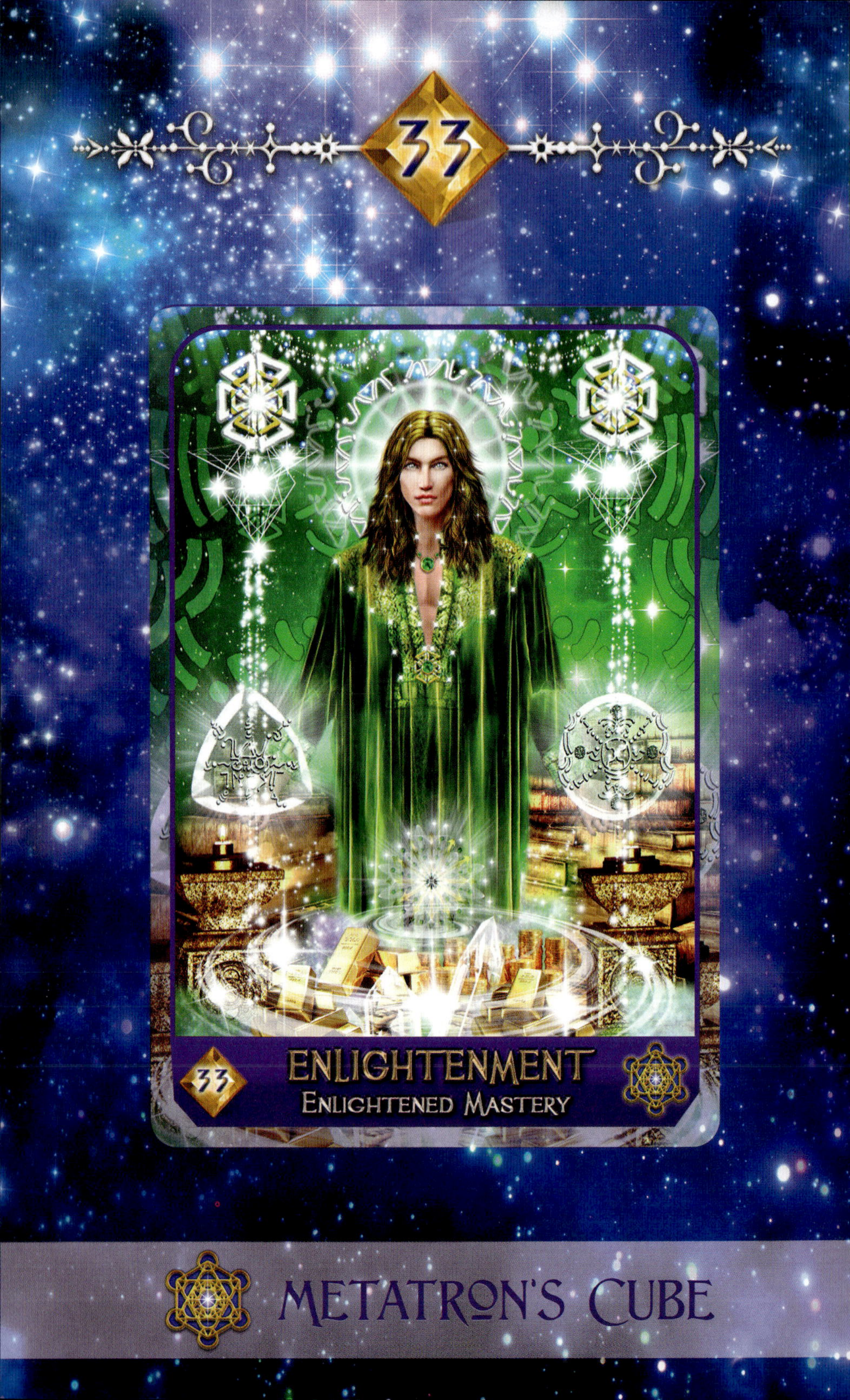

ENLIGHTENMENT
Enlightened Mastery

METATRON'S CUBE

33. ENLIGHTENMENT

Original Artwork Title: *Enlightened Mastery*

THE KEY ENERGIES:

The Ascended Masters are highly advanced souls who have mastered all levels of the third dimension on Earth, over the course of many past incarnations. Through their love for humanity, thoughts, and deeds, they have also chosen to serve as Master Teachers and ascension role models for humanity. Master Hilarion serves as the representing ambassador in this image for all the Ascended Masters as a collective group. These Grand Masters have unsurpassed compassion and love for humanity and carry great wisdom to share with us. They have faced and mastered our same challenges.

THE ORACLE INTERPRETATION:

You are lovingly being guided by the Ascended Masters as your consciousness is upgrading to higher frequencies of love, wisdom, and magnetization energies. This is a powerful time to receive healing dispensations of all levels. Healing Light Codes are being dispersed into your energy to cleanse old patterns of negativity and create new energy templates filled with positivity and love. But first, review all belief systems of scarcity and limitation and transmute these into confidence and empowerment. Learn to harness the Divine wisdom that is already within you. Focus on mastery of your emotions and your environment. You *can* magnetize anything into your life; just remember the power of creation that you carry within your soul.

REALIGNMENTS:

Ascension Mastery; Abundance Visualizations; Ancient Mystery School Training; Ascended Master Connections; Gold and Platinum Metallics; Monoatomic Gold; Colors of Gold and Green; Frankincense and Myrrh Essential Oils; Evening Primrose and Tecoma Flower Essences; Crystals of Citrine, Golden Quartz, and Green Tourmaline

34

COURAGEOUS
Transcending Fear

METATRON'S CUBE

34. COURAGEOUS

Original Artwork Title: *Transcending Fear*

THE KEY ENERGIES:
You are a radiant spark of light, the eternal flame of The Creator. The strength within you is powerful beyond measure. It is immune to darkness and fear and cannot be extinguished. This flame transcends beyond duality. Negative entities do not align with this eternal flame; thus they initiate agendas to dispose of this light in others, but darkness is powerless in the sacred alignment of transcending fear. Choose to shine your divine flame brilliantly and stand firmly rooted and infused with the golden frequency of celestial empowerment.

THE ORACLE INTERPRETATION:
There is a familiar acronym for FEAR: False Evidence Appearing Real. Well, it sure feels real when you are in the thick of it yourself! When you experience fear, there are a few choices you can make. You can either "Forget Everything and Run," or you can "Face Everything and Rise." So ask yourself, "What do I really fear?" Perhaps it is now time to confront your deep-seated or hidden fears. They may be conscious, or imprinted into your subconscious, so be sure to dig deep and be honest with yourself. Clearly decipher the truth that resides at the core of your situation. You may also be absorbing fears of those around you, or in the collective consciousness. Be still and know your power to release lower vibrations, and rise. Align with your inner divine flame and turn that light on full throttle. Your inner faith is being tested right now. Transcend beyond.

REALIGNMENTS:
Empowerment Decrees; Hypnosis; Light Exposure Therapy; Assertiveness Training; Colors of Golden, White, and Red; Lemon and Vetiver Essential Oils; Rock Rose, Scorpion Weed, and Mimulus Flower Essences; Crystals of Yellow Aventurine, Red Jasper, and Pink Dolomite

35

REPAIR
528 Hz Miracles Healing Code

THE HEALING CODES

35. REPAIR

Initiates DNA repair and transformation and promotes empowerment
Associated with the SOLAR PORTAL (Chakra)

> ORIGINAL ARTWORK TITLE: *528 Hz Miracles Healing Code*

(THE HEALING CODE SERIES)

THE KEY ENERGIES:

The Healing Code Series includes potent healing codes that resonate to specific Solfeggio tones and contain visual-activation properties. Solfeggio frequencies make up the ancient six-tone scale thought to have been used in sacred music, including the beautiful and well-known Gregorian chants. The chants and their special tones were believed to impart spiritual blessings when sung in harmony. Each Solfeggio tone is composed of a frequency required to balance your energy and keep your body, mind, and spirit in perfect unison. Experiencing the vibration of these frequencies in the form of visual art enhances these tones, forming an alchemical healing activation for the soul.

THE ORACLE INTERPRETATION:

The Miracles Healing Code resonates to the Solfeggio tone of 528 Hz, which rebalances the energy center of the solar chakra. This potent code aligns with self-confidence and helps with increasing energy in the body. It also assists with DNA repair, so it is perfect for initiating healing upgrades. Linked with high frequencies of transformation and miracles, this means ANYTHING is possible. Now is the time to activate and enhance your physical reality; however, this may indicate that a shift or change is in order. It could take the form of a geographical relocation, a new health regimen, or releasing relationships that are not for your highest and best good. Step forward.

REALIGNMENTS:

Solar Chakra; 528 Hz Solfeggio Tone; DNA Repair Supplements; Rife Frequency Resonator; Orgone; Colors of Turquoise and Mint Green; Celery Seed and Cypress Essential Oils; White Hyacinth and Blue Gromwell Flower Essences; Crystals of Shattuckite, Chrysocolla, and Shungite Stone

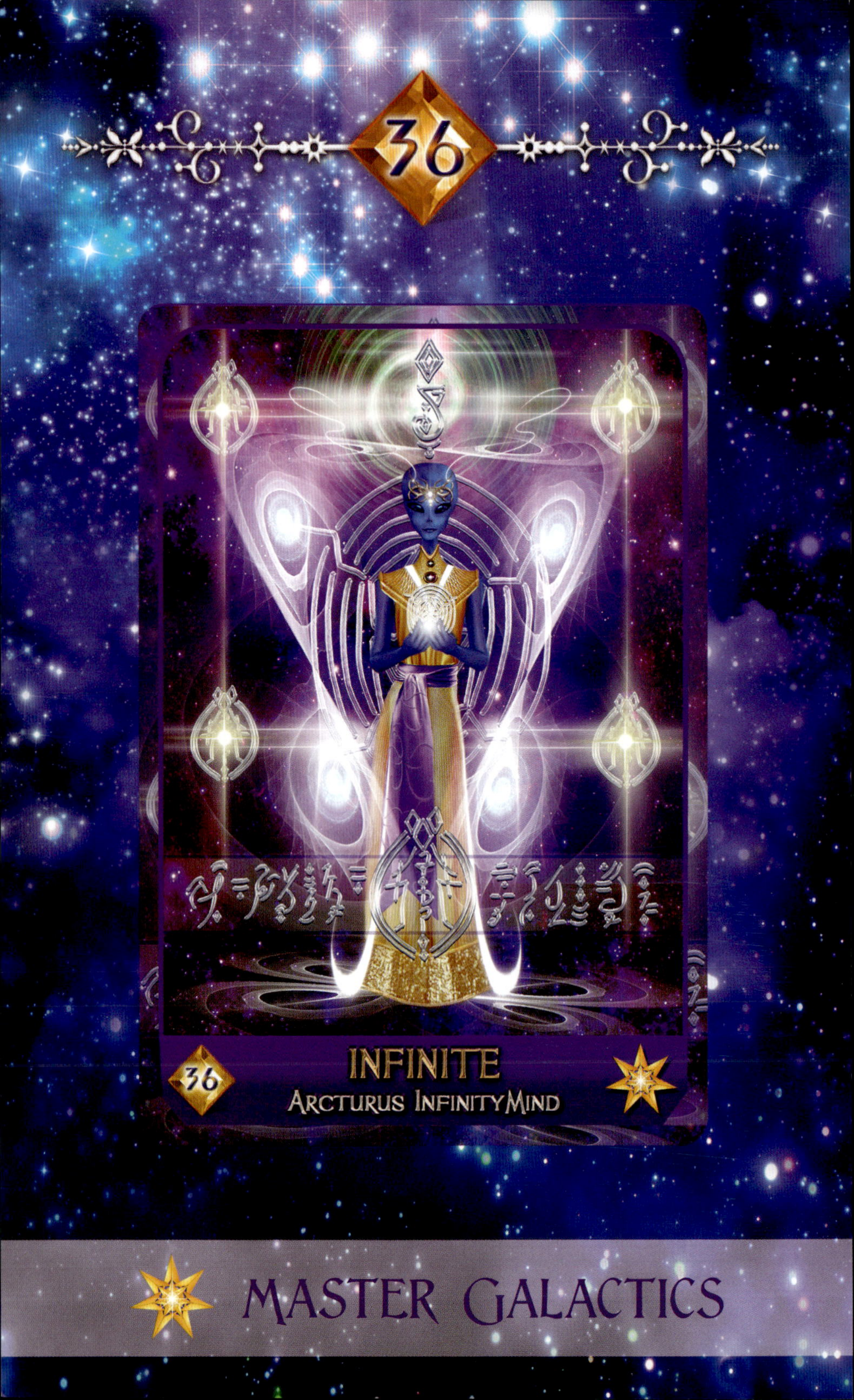
36
36
INFINITE
ARCTURUS INFINITYMIND
MASTER GALACTICS

36. INFINITE

ORIGINAL ARTWORK TITLE: *ARCTURUS INFINITYMIND*

THE KEY ENERGIES:

Blessings to all sentient beings as we generate a high-frequency cascade of luminescence from Arcturus. Travel with us beyond your limitations by transporting your mind on a journey to infinity, where all is possible, and positive mind streams are endless. We assist with dissolving mental thought patterns that become trapped in lower-vibrational matter, clear the negative mind field, and construct new neural pathways to clarity. We help raise frequencies with our InfinityMind.

THE ORACLE INTERPRETATION:

You are being supported by the high vibratory frequencies of the Arcturus InfinityMind. These unique spheres and neuronal circuitry of healing transmit waves of infinitude, which expand your central nervous system and build new neural pathways to promote unlimited thinking. By infusing your energy with luminous light codes, you receive greater clarity, and a sense of well-being and positivity floods into your mental field. It's time to focus and notice if you have been inundated with thoughts that are coated with resistance, lack, or limitation. Release the confines of your mind with a dose of the boundless nature of the true mind of infinite silence. Your attention needs to be focused on expansiveness and clear thinking. Look to old thought patterns that are keeping you from generating creative solutions.

REALIGNMENTS:

Mind-Clearing Meditation; Sacred Geometries of Light; Advanced Light Technologies; Holographic Energies; DNA Upgrades; Colors of Violet and Purple; Ho Wood and Palo Santo Essential Oils; Cosmos and Lavender Flower Essences; Crystals of Purple Fluorite, Amethyst, and Sugilite

37. METAMORPHOSIS

Expands intuition, encourages mental peace, and inspires innovative solutions
Associated with the THIRD-EYE PORTAL (Chakra)

> Original Artwork Title: *852 Hz Clarity Healing Code*

(The Healing Code Series)

THE KEY ENERGIES:

The Healing Code Series includes potent healing codes that resonate to specific Solfeggio tones and contain visual activation properties. Solfeggio frequencies make up the ancient six-tone scale thought to have been used in sacred music, including the beautiful and well-known Gregorian chants. The chants and their special tones were believed to impart spiritual blessings when sung in harmony. Each Solfeggio tone is composed of a frequency required to balance your energy and keep your body, mind, and spirit in perfect unison. Experiencing the vibration of these frequencies in the form of visual art enhances these tones, forming an alchemical healing activation for the soul.

THE ORACLE INTERPRETATION:

The Clarity Healing Code resonates to the Solfeggio tone of 852 Hz, which balances the energy center of the third-eye chakra. This motivational code helps restore a sense of clarity, initiates positive change, clears the subconscious mind of negative thought patterns, and enhances your intuition. This power code amplifies transformation of limiting thoughts and belief systems and encourages a return to clear thinking with enhanced ESP. Reengage with an outlook of optimism. Shift your thoughts in the now moment, to the highest potentiality, and know that you are the change you wish to see.

REALIGNMENTS:

Third-Eye Chakra; 852 Hz Solfeggio Tone; Jedi Training; Meditation; ESP Training; Martial Arts; Subliminal Music; Colors of Purple, Violet, and Silver; Blue Lotus and Peppermint Essential Oils; Purple Monkeyflower and Lavender Flower Essences; Crystals of Lepidolite, Purple Agate, and Iolite

38

INTEGRATION
Higher Self Integration

METATRON'S CUBE

38. INTEGRATION

ORIGINAL ARTWORK TITLE: *HIGHER SELF INTEGRATION*

THE KEY ENERGIES:

In the multidimensional spectrum of the soul, therein resides a harmonious clarity, a pure expression of divine love, and a source of infinite wisdom. It is within the energy of this divine spirit that knows only truth and contains the highest echelons of light. It is here where you can discover a connection with your higher self, and the unity consciousness that is blended with the All-That-Is. A powerhouse source of knowledge, and the golden codes from which truth is dispensed. Amid any chaos, you will find only peace, wholeness, and clarity in this sacredness . . . expansive, enlightened, and free.

THE ORACLE INTERPRETATION:

Integration with your higher self is a natural process of spiritual enlightenment. That familiar saying "All answers reside within" is not just a mere cliché; it is the direct truth. Although we all encounter many distractions in life that foster separation from your higher self, you will always receive ample opportunities and gentle nudges to reconnect with that part of your soul that holds unparalleled clarity and wisdom. If you have not been hearing your higher self's wisdom, you must quiet your mind and expand your consciousness. Listen to the subtle voice and intuitive promptings that will not just tell you what you want to hear, but rather the truth infused with love. Your answers reside in this precious place. Embrace your ever-present divine connection.

REALIGNMENTS:

Higher Self-Meditations; Channeled Journaling; Sunlight; Lightbody Activation; Practicing Mirror Work; Colors of Gold and Rose; Pink Lotus and Rose Essential Oils; Pink Oleander; Golden Sunflower and Bird of Paradise Flower Essences; Crystals of Golden Topaz, Diamond, and Rose Aura Quartz

39 TRANSMUTATION
Cellular Intelligence

METATRON'S CUBE

39. Transmutation

Original Artwork Title: *Cellular Intelligence*

THE KEY ENERGIES:

Every cell in the human physical body has its own intelligence and innate wisdom. When you experience trauma, whether it be physical, mental, emotional, or spiritual, negative energy vibrations can become stored in the cellular memory. If these vibrations are not acknowledged and cleared, the cellular reservoirs become overly saturated, which can cause disruption in our field of well-being. It is essential to purify our memory channels, so we can be free to flourish and thrive.

THE ORACLE INTERPRETATION:

It will serve you well to incorporate some tender loving care toward yourself in all ways. Engage in any form of healing that purifies the body, mind, emotions, and spirit. Explore the realms of cellular renewal. Toxic emotions, negative thinking, or a less-than-optimal state of health will need to be addressed from a multilevel approach right now. If you're feeling mentally taxed, relaxation is in order. If you've been lazy with self-care, it is vital that you place your attention back on your well-being. Your cells await your love and healing. You also have healing abilities that wish to be activated. You may be ready to engage in some new healing modalities. Use these gifts for your own self-healing, and also to help others.

REALIGNMENTS:

Reiki Healing; DNA Activation; Crystal Healing; Cellular Detoxification; Orb Healing; Past-Life Therapy; Hydrotherapy; Colors of Deep Blue, Pink, and White; Celery Seed and Clove Essential Oils; Nasturtium and Impatiens Flower Essences; Crystals of Clear Quartz, All Colored Fluorites, and Seraphinite

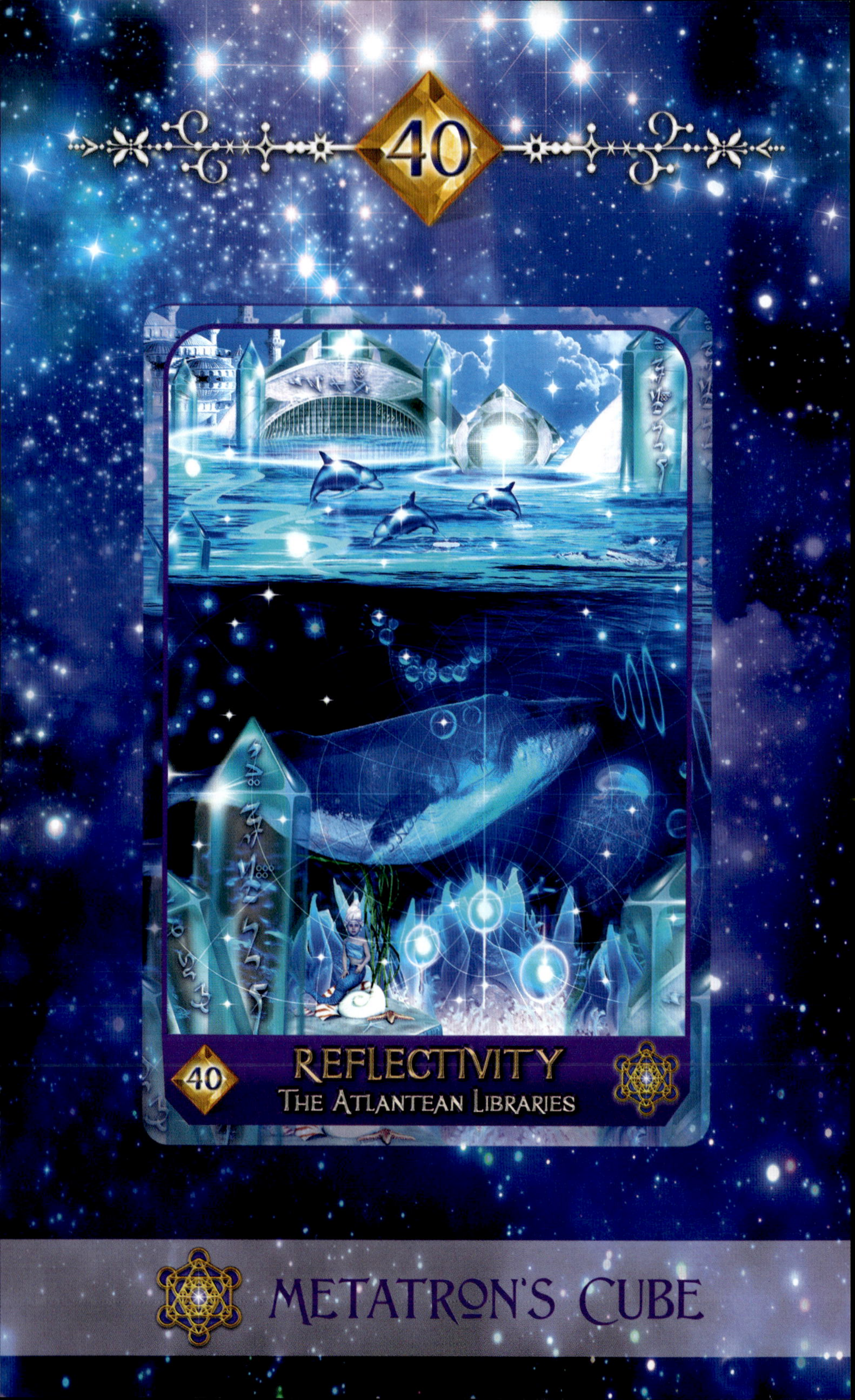

40

REFLECTIVITY
The Atlantean Libraries

METATRON'S CUBE

40. REFLECTIVITY

Original Artwork Title: *The Atlantean Libraries* (Panoramic)

THE KEY ENERGIES:

Within the matrix of the soul therein resides innate abilities to access information, memories, and realities that have occurred in all past, present, and future timelines, coinciding within one access point. This centric point of contact is key for what is known as accessing the Akashic Records, where all knowledge that has ever been is stored. Data from personal, universal, or cosmic Akasha can be acquired from the soul, with expansive capabilities of reaching all access points with varying degrees of clearance. This data bank is infused in several locations: from Source Creation, and within soul matrices, planetary core vortex zones, gridular leylines, and energetic DNA-encoded material.

THE ORACLE INTERPRETATION:

Prepare yourself for a psychic expedition into the realms of the Akasha! But have patience; you may need to wait just a wee bit longer before you depart. There are a few unconscious hidden truths that need to be addressed first. Your voyage involves others, so a visit to the Akashic Records will provide valuable insight. Call upon the mighty ocean whales to assist you with accessing the Akasha, so you can download glimpses and flashes of insight to help you decipher your situation more clearly. Be open to perceiving the whole picture, and not just pieces of the puzzle. You will soon understand the adhesive bond that binds it all together. You may wish to postpone taking immediate action, just until you have more information. This will ultimately help you make more-enlightened decisions on this matter.

REALIGNMENTS:

Akashic Records Readings; Past-Life Regression; Sonic Whale Tones; Dolphin Communication; Crystal Programming; Celtic Sea Salt Therapies; Colors of Sea-Foam and Arctic Blue; White Spruce and Fragonia Essential Oils; Black Locust and Crown-of-Thorns Flower Essences; Crystals of Blue Calcite and Dumortierite

41

UNIFICATION
963 Hz Oneness Healing Code

THE HEALING CODES

41. UNIFICATION

Connects with the Divine Creator and ignites unity consciousness
Associated with the CROWN PORTAL (Chakra)

Original Artwork Title: *963 Hz Oneness Healing Code*

(The Healing Code Series)

THE KEY ENERGIES:

The Healing Code Series includes potent healing codes that resonate to specific Solfeggio tones and contain visual-activation properties. Solfeggio frequencies make up the ancient six-tone scale thought to have been used in sacred music, including the beautiful and well-known Gregorian chants. The chants and their special tones were believed to impart spiritual blessings when sung in harmony. Each Solfeggio tone is composed of a frequency required to balance your energy and keep your body, mind, and spirit in perfect unison. Experiencing the vibration of these frequencies in the form of visual art enhances these tones, forming an alchemical healing activation for the soul.

THE ORACLE INTERPRETATION:

The Oneness Healing Code resonates to the Solfeggio tone of 963 Hz, which balances the energy center of the crown chakra. This brilliant code connects with cellular enlightenment and unity consciousness and activates the pineal gland to its highest echelon. Connect with these energies and you will inevitably invoke your highest pureness. Be open to receiving access to the infinite cosmic energy matrix, All-That-Is, which is intimately unified with spiritual oneness. Recall the perfection in ALL situations, and know that everything is in divine timing, and for divine purpose. Relax—all is well!

REALIGNMENTS:

Third-Eye Chakra; 963 Hz Solfeggio Tone; Angelic Music; the Om 432 Frequency; Pineal-Gland Activation; Colors of Pink, Gold, and White; Pearly Everlasting and Pink Daffodil Flower Essences; White and Pink Lotus Essential Oils; Crystals of Selenite, Moonstone, and Pink Kunzite

42

COLLABORATION
The Alliance

MASTER GALACTICS

42. COLLABORATION

Original Artwork Title: *The Alliance*

THE KEY ENERGIES:
We are light. We are love. We are you. We represent the strength and matrix of those who serve in the many universes and dimensions and embody high vibrations of integrity, love, and wisdom. We are not the royalty of the ages but, rather, serve in the trenches, "down to Earth," to build the bridge toward the Alliance of spiritual oneness and peace. We are the reminder of Divine Light embodied within all of you. We work cohesively together to forge new pathways for peace, deliver clarity and insight, initiate courageousness, and serve as the inspirational reminder of your great capacity for expanding into higher frequencies of love. You are us; we are you. We are One.

THE ORACLE INTERPRETATION:
You are not alone in your endeavors, and The Alliance is here to remind you of the support and comradery that now exists all around you. Evaluate your life and notice where you tend to "fly solo." Not that there's anything wrong with being the Lone Ranger, however; sometimes we all need a helping hand. Do not be afraid of asking for assistance; drop the excess baggage and burdens from your shoulders. You may also be ready for new connections with your cosmic soul group, star family, someone new, or a group project. Those who may be entering your life soon will have a great and positive impact on you, so be open to conscious collaboration with others. Unity consciousness will greatly benefit your life.

REALIGNMENTS:
Group Meditations and Classes; Socializing with Friends; Volunteer Work; Focusing on Mission/Purpose; Cedarwood Smudging; Green Tea Incense; Colors of Leafy Green, White, and Purple; Vanilla and Coriander Essential Oils; Elm and Chicory Flower Essences; Crystals of Dioptase and Purple Tanzanite

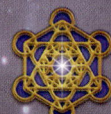

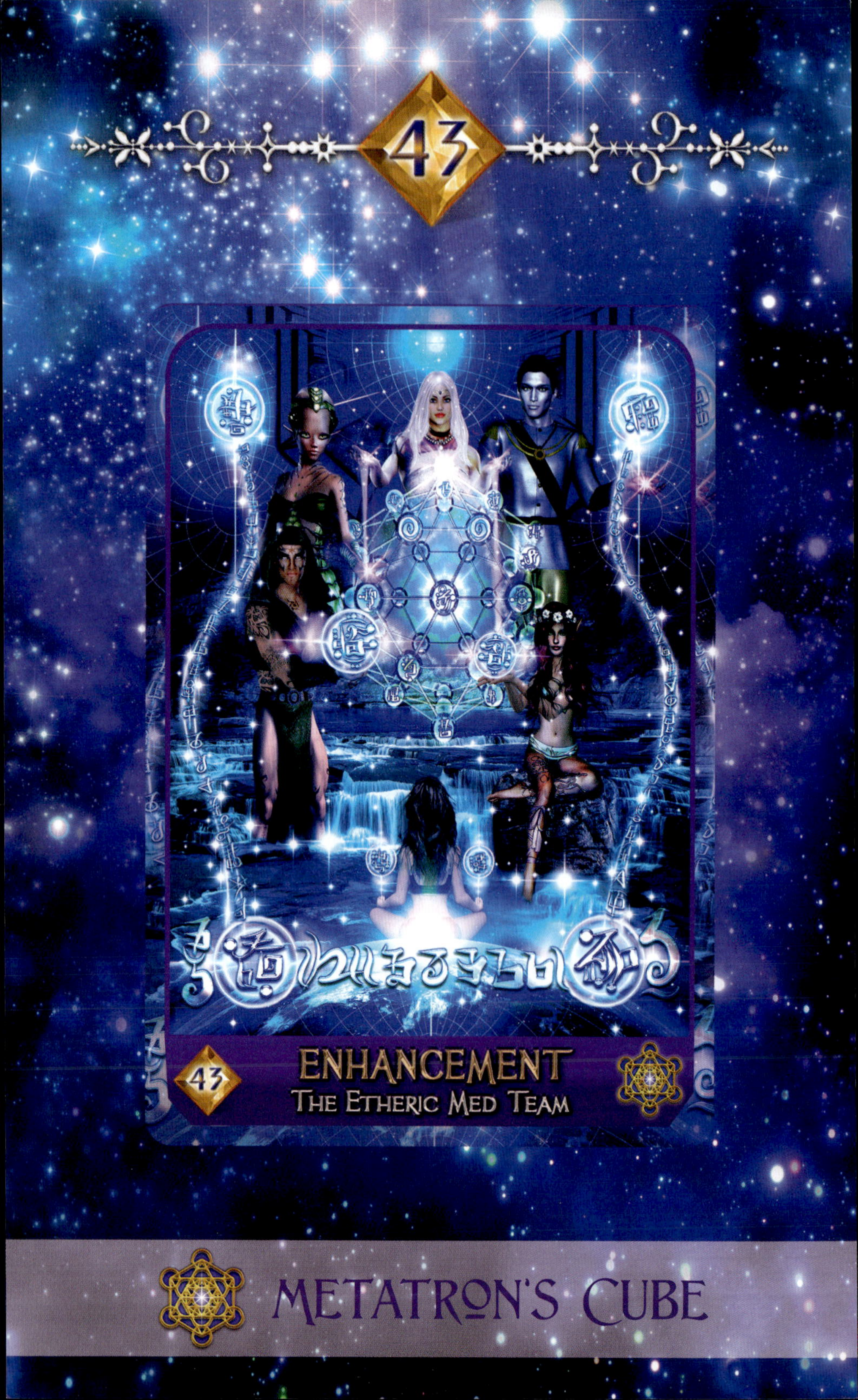
43
43
ENHANCEMENT
THE ETHERIC MED TEAM
METATRON'S CUBE

43. ENHANCEMENT

Original Artwork Title: *The Etheric Med Team*

THE KEY ENERGIES:

The vast realms of healing are within your reach. Merely engaging clear focus and connection to these realms, shall you find us beyond the veil, and that which you seek will be given. Our hearts are filled with purity and love; we assist all those in need. We reside on starships, on planetary biospheres, in the astral plane, and in alternate dimensional realities, and each one of you has access to connecting with us. Working in unison, in tandem with one another is our mantra, to provide the highest level of service to humanity. We are your Med Team, offering our wellness expertise to assist with your ultimate healing success.

THE ORACLE INTERPRETATION:

You are not alone in your quest for healing and clarity. Access higher levels of assistance in this very moment; your Etheric Med Team awaits your call. Struggling with a health challenge? Your Wellness Team can help guide you to solutions for your particular concern. Having trouble receiving intuitive guidance, or have you been given the runaround by the third-dimensional medical field? You now have an opportunity to receive a fresh perspective. Gain clarity from your Wellness Team's healing guidance on all levels; physical, emotional, mental, or spiritual issues. It might also be time for a personal upgrade or recalibration from your team. So, tune into your etheric healing experts, to provide innovative new action steps to enhance your situation.

REALIGNMENTS:

Sacred Geometry Healing; Light Language Activation; Etheric and Astral Healing; Telepathic Communication; Colors of Periwinkle and Silvery Blue; Eucalyptus and Blue Spruce Essential Oils; Self-Heal, Bluestar, and Rock Rose Flower Essences; Crystals of Rainbow Fluorite and Blue Topaz

44

RECEPTIVITY
Angelic Diamond Light

METATRON'S CUBE

44. RECEPTIVITY

ORIGINAL ARTWORK TITLE: *ANGELIC DIAMOND LIGHT*

THE KEY ENERGIES:

Within the Angelic Realms, therein resides such incredible support. Angelic energy is like being immersed in a waterfall of love. Some Angels carry vibrations that allow them to incarnate into physical form, and yet others are pure energy. There is as much variety as the stars. However, we all contain specific codes within our matrix that emanate The Creator's powerful frequencies. We, the Angelic Collective, serve as messengers, healers, and support for all sentient beings. Whether you need inspiration to lift depression, support for healing, or a boost of positivity . . . we are here, always loving, and loving in all ways.

THE ORACLE INTERPRETATION:

The Angels are here to lighten and brighten your pathway from heaviness, darkness, or shadows. The Angelics invite you to be in the present moment and tune in. Are you listening to their guidance? Be empowered by stepping forward into your highest light. Remember who you really are, a beautiful spark of the divine. Choose to be that brilliantly filled vessel of love. Initiate potent Angel codes and embed them into all areas of your life. Love is always the answer, so if your situation involves inner conflict, or challenges with others, express yourself with peace in your heart, and shower Angel inspirations on the matter. Envelope yourself in Diamond Angelic Light Codes. Herald in the Angels for strength and guidance as a healing balm, and know that you are receiving assistance in this very moment.

REALIGNMENTS:

Aromatherapy; Angel Healing; Angelic Tarot or Oracle Cards; Reiki Healing; Colors of Blue, White, and Pink; Gardenia Flower, Jasmine, and Angelica Essential Oils; Honeysuckle and Hyacinth Flower Essences; Crystals of Celestite, Angelite, and Apophyllite